A Proven Path to a

PROFITABLE LAW PRACTICE

ONE
OF A
BY *Jay Harrington*
KIND

HARRINGTON

ONE REALLY GOOD IDEA EVERY DAY
attorneyatwork @

For my lovely (and patient) wife, Heather, and our three little ladies, Maddie, Emma and Kinsey.

CONTENTS

ABOUT THE AUTHOR

 **Jay Harrington** is an attorney and graduate of the University of Michigan Law School. He practiced law as a commercial litigator and corporate bankruptcy attorney at international law firms Skadden, Arps, Slate, Meagher & Flom and Foley & Lardner. He also cofounded a boutique corporate bankruptcy firm in metro Detroit focused on automotive restructuring.

Jay now runs Harrington, a brand strategy and content marketing agency that helps lawyers and law firms across the country increase market awareness and improve business development efforts (www.hcommunications.biz). He also coaches and consults with individual attorneys and groups of attorneys on a number of issues, including personal brand development, niching strategy and content marketing strategy. He also writes and speaks frequently on these and other topics.

Jay lives in beautiful Traverse City, Michigan, with his wife and three young daughters, and he enjoys hiking, biking, paddle boarding, golfing and skiing.

Jay writes about issues of importance to lawyers and law firms on his agency's blog, Simply Stated.

AKNOWLEDGMENTS

I would like to express my gratitude to the people who supported me while I completed this book; from those who offered comments and suggestions, to attorneys who spoke to me regarding their personal experiences, to the talented people who assisted in the editing, proofreading and design.

Thank you to Merrilyn Astin Tarlton and Joan Feldman for their encouragement and support during this process, and for holding the hand of a first-time author. I greatly appreciate the opportunities you have provided me to write this book, and to share perspectives on www.AttorneyatWork.com.

I'm grateful to Timothy Johnson for his keen insights and sharp eye. It was a pleasure to work with you, and you added tremendous value to the book, both with what you suggested I add and (especially) with what you had me take out.

And thank you to my wife, Heather, who put up with me during law school and my legal career, and — just when she thought she was free of it — now during the process of writing a book for lawyers. Thank you for your unending support.

INTRODUCTION

Taking the first step toward a worthwhile destination is a curiously — and often maddeningly — difficult thing to do. Starting is hard.

If you are reading this, you started something hard, or are about to: your legal career. I did that once as well. But I stopped and pivoted to a career of advising lawyers instead of being one. A legal career as a practicing lawyer wasn't for me (or perhaps I wasn't for it). So I applaud you for your commitment and perseverance. It can be a great career. I've seen it. I know many who love it and excel at it. You likely do, too. Perhaps you're one of them.

But perhaps not. Maybe something is missing. You may not be able to put your finger on it, but it's not what you imagined.

Come on, admit it. Your early impressions of what it would be like to practice law were formed just like they were for the rest of us — from pop culture. John Grisham novels, Perry Mason thrillers, "L.A. Law" drama. It seemed so glamorous. And easy.

But, of course, it's not easy. We've all been through the drill. You graduate law school and, if you're fortunate enough to land a job, you quickly get thrown into a situation you're largely unprepared for. OK, that's putting it too mildly. More like thrown into a whirlwind. The hours are rough. Clients are challenging. You're forced to deal with adversaries on the other side, and perhaps even at your firm. The learning curve is steep, and most lawyers are forced to climb it alone. At times it's jarringly difficult.

Pretty soon, though, you get your feet underneath you and settle in. You learn the fundamentals and can function within the system. You no longer fear the phone ringing, and you don't break out in a cold sweat at the thought of a court appearance. I remember the dread I felt every time the flashing red light on my desktop phone or Blackberry signaled the arrival of a new voicemail or email. The terror passes. It may have taken a few years, but now there's a certain comfort and satisfaction derived from achieving competent practitioner status. Phase One of your journey is over. So what's next? It's time to transition from being a lawyer to building a practice.

For most, this is a big step. Many never get there. For some, it's lack of effort. For others, it's lack of direction. For those who lack motivation, well, there's not much that can be done. Either you've got it or you don't. There's no coach that's going to be tugging on your face mask or giving "rah-rah" pep talks on this playing field.

Aimlessness, on the other hand, can be remedied. Ironically, many lack direction — in all fields and endeavors — not from too little information, but from too much. Like waves crashing onshore, our inboxes and social media feeds are relentlessly bombarded with advice, strategies and tactics for self-improvement.

We end up consuming so much professional improvement advice that we never get around to implementing any of it effectively. One day we're told to compile our daily to-do list first thing in the morning, the next day we're advised to do so at night. And so on. I mean, if there are "20 Things That Top Business Leaders Do Before 6 A.M.," there must be a hundred more we should be adopting in the subsequent 12 hours, right?

The point is that we end up changing up our routine so frequently that it never becomes habitual. Information overload is one of the primary reasons (along with lack of discipline) that there is often a huge gap between our understanding of what we should be doing (our knowledge) and what we actually do (our actions).

So I pose a challenge to you: Learn less, do more.

While learning feels good — and it is good — it's often a crutch that keeps us from moving forward. To do something hard, the essential first step is action.

But if you need a foundation for action, I urge you to keep reading. There is no single path to a successful law practice. Over time, paths become blocked and new ones emerge. What worked 10 years ago may not work today. What works for some will not work for others. It's said that business development is a relationship game. That's true, and likely always will be. But the manner in which meaningful, beneficial client relationships are formed and sustained is constantly evolving.

This book identifies, describes and distills the common characteristics and tactics of lawyers who have built interesting, profitable practices, and it provides a path for others to follow in their footsteps. I'm not suggesting that it's the only path. Surely it isn't. But it's one that has worked — in many cases spectacularly well — for some of the best lawyers in the business. And it can work for you, too. At its core, the purpose of this book is to help you change your mindset, and more importantly your actions, so that you can take control of your legal career, rather than let it control you. Remember, your legal career is not what it is today: It's what you make it tomorrow.

PART ONE

A ONE-OF-A-KIND MINDSET

1

SAME IS NOT A STRATEGY

Have you ever put yourself in a prospective client's shoes?
Why would he, she or it hire you? Seriously, why? I'm sure you're
a good lawyer, but (1) how would a prospective client know that
and (2), perhaps more importantly, can most prospective clients,
at the point of purchase, discern between an average lawyer and
a good one, or even a great one?

Consciously or not, most lawyers make a choice to craft professional
personas that are largely indistinguishable from others. From their new
business pitch to their website bio, they purposefully look, sound, act and
describe themselves in a similar manner. This poses a dilemma for clients:
When confronted with a commodity, how to make a choice?

The paradox is that sellers of actual commodities do the exact opposite of
lawyers: They compete fiercely on grocers' shelves to stand out from their
competition. Sellers of actual commodities know that only by standing out
can they capture a greater share of market.

That's not to suggest that lawyers are commodities. There are good
lawyers and there are bad lawyers. Young and old. Ethical and unethical.
Serious and quirky. Introverts and extroverts. The profession teems with
professionals of wildly different backgrounds, experience and expertise.
Having the benefit of near daily interactions with other lawyers, those in
the business can quickly and easily discern between someone who is the
real deal and a wannabe. But while the reputation you earn among your

colleagues is undoubtedly important, the ultimate challenge is convincing the client — the one who signs the checks — of your worth.

When it comes to standing out, same is not a strategy.

Information Overload

Self-inflicted commoditization in legal services is increasing, at a time when stark differentiation is more relevant than ever. Consumers of legal services have more choices than ever, and they are being bombarded with information, largely indistinguishable, about those choices. Many are simply tuning out.

There was a time when a Chambers listing or Martindale-Hubbell "AV" rating meant something. Now there's Super Lawyers, The Best Lawyers in America, US News & World Report, Go-To Law Firm, Avvo — the list of ratings service providers goes on and on. State and local publications have jumped on the rankings gravy train, too, publishing annual lists and selling ads to honorees. In my hometown of Detroit, which is not a big legal market, at least two print business magazines publish "top lawyer" lists on an annual basis. That's on top of all of the national publications and ranking services. Everyone and every firm seem to be on a list, if not multiple ones.

Clients are also suffering from information overload as a result of the crush of newsletters, alerts, blog, social media posts and other outbound communications being pumped out by lawyers and law firms. It's not that the tactic is wrong, it's that the information itself is often not that helpful. And even if it is, it's getting lost in the shuffle.

Marketing firm Greentarget conducts an annual survey called the "State of Digital and Content Marketing Survey," which asks questions of in-house counsel and firm marketing leaders about their content consumption and production habits and intentions. In recent years, the survey has shown that while the amount of information produced by firms and the number of channels through which firms are distributing information have increased, the appetite of in-house counsel for that information may be waning.

For example, the 2014 survey indicated that blogs published by AmLaw 200 firms increased from approximately 350 in 2010 to approximately 1,000 in 2014. During the same time period, however, in-house counsel blog readership dropped. According to the survey, 46 percent of in-house counsel followed a legal blog in 2013, but that number decreased to 38 percent in 2014. The survey's authors suggest that in spite of the increase in published and distributed information, readership levels have declined because of content oversaturation.

Clients are tuning out the traditional methods of overture.

The Market Is Flat (and Changing)

Remember the good old days? The days when hourly rates increased year after year, junior associate time could be billed for, and it was considered unprofessional to try to poach another lawyer's clients? That wasn't that long ago, in fact. But times have changed.

The market for legal services is flat. Since the Great Recession, there has been fundamental change in the legal landscape. Much like the housing market bubble that precipitated the economic slowdown, the legal marketplace has shifted from a seller's to a buyer's market. This has led to downward pressure on fees, increased demand for creative, alternative billing practices, and greater competition for fewer opportunities. Work has also moved in-house, as corporate law departments have looked for ways to cut outside spending and beef up internal talent and resources.

Sensing this shift, non-lawyer entrepreneurs have stepped into the legal services marketplace. From overseas document review firms to Silicon Valley technology startups, alternative legal service providers continue to chip away at work that traditionally was within the exclusive domain of lawyers and law firms. Much of this work kept junior lawyers busy and billing. Companies such as LegalZoom and Rocket Lawyer, which were once seen as novelties, continue to encroach on the turf of solo practitioners and small law firms.

As other industries have experienced — from retail to music, software to automotive — the legal industry is experiencing change both more rapid and more profound than most could have predicted even just 15 years ago.

There's valid debate concerning the extent of these pressures, and whether they represent short-term challenges or long-term fundamental changes. These challenges were addressed in a *Harvard Business Review* article by Clayton Christensen, Dina Wang and Derek van Bever entitled "Consulting on the Cusp of Disruption." In it, the authors argue that providers of professional services — including, yes, law firms — are no more immune to disruption than other industries:

> We have come to the conclusion that the same forces that disrupted so many businesses, from steel to publishing, are starting to reshape the world of consulting. The implications for firms and their clients are significant. The pattern of industry disruption is familiar: New competitors with new business models arrive; incumbents choose to ignore the new players or to flee to higher-margin activities; a disrupter whose product was once barely good enough achieves a level of quality acceptable to the broad middle of the market, undermining the position of longtime leaders and often causing the "flip" to a new basis of competition. (Available at https://hbr .org/2013/10/consulting-on-the-cusp-of-disruption.)

Certainly, many lawyers and law firms have excelled, and will continue to excel, in this "new normal" environment. There will always be winners and losers. But more often than not, the winners are not standing on the podium by accident. They have made some change, reinvented their approach, and taken some action to arrive there.

The Fool's Gold of Full Service

The changes made and actions taken by "winners" (however fleeting and sometimes unsatisfying that designation may be) vary greatly. There's not one path to greatness. But one thing is clear — most have not gotten there by acting more similar to their competitors. "Full-service" law firms struggle to define any meaningful points of differentiation from their competitors. The individual lawyer equivalent of the "full-service" firm, the "generalist," faces the same challenge.

It's not that being a well-rounded lawyer is a bad thing. A lawyer with depth and breadth of knowledge is obviously a valuable asset to a client. It's that positioning oneself as providing "full service" or possessing "general knowledge" is often ineffective. This is about more than semantics.

In all aspects of today's economy, consumers are trending toward specialization. In the medical field, the family and general practitioner's office is often just the first stop — often mandated by insurance coverage — on the way to the specialist. The full-service advertising agency model of the "Mad Men" era continues to be usurped by agencies focusing on narrow industries and service specializations. Many advertising clients are no longer seeking an "agency of record," but rather the best agency to help with a specific project intended to achieve a specific objective. IT and software consultants are developing solutions not for mass markets, but for industries — from healthcare to financial services — that face common challenges.

These changes are happening in response to market demands — consumers are no longer looking for service providers with broad skill sets; instead, consumers are seeking out specialists with very particular knowledge in industries and market segments. Narrow and deep, not broad and shallow, is what clients value.

The legal industry is not immune from these trends. Large, full-service firms are facing increasing competition from smaller, boutique specialist firms. In some instances, price is a factor, as a smaller firm can often charge less or offer a more flexible alternative fee arrangement than its larger competitors. But in many cases the boutique specialist firm is successful not because it charges less, but rather because it is able to harness all of its energy — from marketing to creative work product — to address the unique challenges faced by a particular segment of the market. Price is not a factor, at least not a primary one.

Specialization is what's driving the buying decision, particularly for "bet the company" type engagements.

While it's not easy to offer fewer options to the marketplace, trying to please everyone makes the options you do offer far less appealing. As journalist and author Herbert Bayard Swope wisely noted, "I can't give you a sure-fire formula for success, but I can give you a formula for failure: try to please everybody all the time."

Good News and Bad News

As in any marketplace experiencing rapid change, there is good news and bad news for market participants. While those who fail to adapt to change will fall further behind, those who embrace it will have new, exciting opportunities. Indeed, this is no time for inaction. It's time for innovation.

Capitalizing on these opportunities, however, requires commitment. Commitment to change. Commitment to creative thinking. And commitment to long-term strategic action, not simply planning, that involves establishing one's expertise, building one's personal brand, embracing one's clients, and confidently and consistently projecting one's unique value and thought leadership to the marketplace. Each of these strategic actions will be explored in subsequent chapters. In Chapter 2, we begin by examining the importance of creativity, and how harnessing one's creative thinking is a fundamental building block to building a successful practice.

2

THE CREATIVE LAWYER (NOT AN OXYMORON)

In a changing world, says LinkedIn cofounder Reid Hoffman, "Playing it safe is one of the riskiest things you can do." That's because while you're standing still, change is happening all around you.

If you accept the premise that we are in a time of radical change in the legal industry (if you don't, please think again), then the natural follow-up question is: What are most lawyers and law firms doing to adapt? Very little, unfortunately. Most are playing it safe, hunkering down and waiting to see how things "shake out."

The wait-and-see approach, while misguided, is not surprising. There's no swift, immediate crisis hammering the industry. It's more of a slow creep. And in this environment there are many firms and lawyers that are still thriving. There are also barriers to entry that will keep many non-traditional competitors at bay.

But there are wide gaps between those who are thriving and those who are simply surviving. An individual lawyer who approaches her practice in the same manner, with the same mindset, that she did 20 or even 10 years ago is likely feeling left behind. She may not be able to pinpoint what has changed, but if she is honest with herself she'll realize that what hasn't changed is her approach to business. She has failed to think creatively about how to move her practice forward.

Lawyers and Creativity

Saying that lawyers aren't creative is like saying that the sky is blue. It's not controversial, but it doesn't tell the whole story.

Just as it's inaccurate to describe a sunrise as "blue" when the sky is radiating pink, purple, red, yellow and orange, all lawyers should not be lumped into some indistinguishable uncreative heap. Sure, excellent lawyers are valued for sharp analytical skills, logical thinking and attention to detail. But the best lawyers are those who are also able to craft creative solutions. That's because it takes creativity to solve a problem.

According to developmental psychologist Howard Gardner:

> People are creative when they can solve problems, create products, or raise issues in a domain in a way that is initially novel but is eventually accepted in one or more cultural settings. Similarly, a work is creative if it stands out at first in terms of its novelty but ultimately comes to be accepted within a domain. The acid test of creativity is simple: In the wake of a putatively creative work, has the domain subsequently been changed? (Howard Gardner, *Intelligence Reframed: Multiple Intelligences for the 21st Century*, 116-17. New York: Basic Books, 1999).

From "poison pills" to bankruptcy "pre-packs," lawyers have crafted many creative solutions to legal challenges that have "changed the domain." Creativity is one of the most important tools in a lawyer's work product toolkit. Unfortunately, most fail to apply the same sort of creative thinking they use when it comes to their work to their marketing and business development activity.

Lawyers' resistance to innovation and creativity is driven by multiple factors. One is risk aversion. I hear it all the time when working with lawyers on brand strategy or website projects: "What are our competitors doing?" It's a great question, but it's typically asked for the wrong reason. Most who pose it are more interested in staying with the pack than breaking away from it.

Another factor is improper perspective or understanding. Many think of creativity as a rare skill possessed by those who come up with big, breakthrough ideas — visionaries such as Steve Jobs, for example. Others believe creativity only applies to those with artistic talents. But creativity comes in all sizes. It's something that can — and should — be applied to any field that engages the mind.

Creativity scholars distinguish between "Big C" creativity and "Small c" creativity. "Big C" creativity is the breakthrough kind of thinking that most people associate with "creative thinkers" such as Jobs and Thomas Edison, but it's rare.

"Small c" creativity, on the other hand, describes the seemingly small ideas that can make a big difference in our lives, like a new organization system at home or project management system at work. A single "Small c" idea won't bring fame or fortune, but lots of them will, over time, lead to incremental advances and daily improvements. And the best way to come up with a "Big C" breakthrough is to cultivate "Small c" thinking on a daily basis.

Creativity, therefore, is not about talent or some flash of inspiration. It's about showing up and doing the work. It's about developing a creativity habit. We're all inherently creative. We just need to be creative.

Overcoming Inertia

That's not to say that it's easy to be a creative lawyer. Logical, rather than creative, thinking is ingrained in us from the beginning of our careers. From law school to law firms, lawyers are taught to think vertically, and work through a problem to a single solution. Lateral thinking, which involves coming at a problem from many different angles, doesn't come as naturally for most. But it's the type of thinking that is required for creative breakthroughs.

And there's a lot of inertia — reluctance to change — in the legal industry. "Different" is frowned upon. Experimentation without judgment is rare. "Worrying" is a state of mind. Firms are managed by partners with differing views and committees that are slow to act.

"Creativity is more than just being different. Anybody can plan weird; that's easy. What's hard is to be as simple as Bach. Making the simple, awesomely simple, that's creativity" — Charles Mingus

But that doesn't mean individual lawyers must follow suit. Once you've embraced the idea that creativity is not a skill or attribute reserved for "special" people, start putting it into practice in order to build your practice.

To become a one-of-a-kind lawyer, it is critical that you nurture your creative side. You may be apprehensive about thinking and acting creatively. That's natural. You may assume you're not creative. That's common. There are many ways to express your creativity, but there's one surefire way not to: Doing nothing. You'll never know what innovative ideas reside within you unless you try.

Start small. Take some risks. By harnessing your creativity, you'll stand apart from the pack. And in the legal industry (naysayers be damned) that's a good thing. By embracing change, and bucking the status quo, you have the power to create an interesting and profitable practice that makes you indispensable, rather than expendable, in the minds of clients. You can go from being one of many to being one of a kind.

PUT CREATIVITY INTO PRACTICE

The practice of law is hard and stressful. The daily rigors and grind can sap creativity, rather than cultivate it. Lawyers need to be proactive and take steps to nurture their creative side.

1. Carve out creative time. Corporate America has long recognized the value of creative thinking, and the need to encourage it. Google, for example, has trumpeted its "20% time" policy — which allows engineers to take one day per week to work on innovative side projects — as key to its ability to innovate. So, carve out dedicated time each week for creative thinking. Try to do this creative thinking offsite so that you are away from the distractions of the office.

Creative brainstorming sessions with colleagues — no smartphones or negativity allowed — are also a key catalyst for coming up with marketing and business development solutions. When was the last time that you spent an hour in a conference room with nothing but a whiteboard and some whip-smart people trying to figure out a better way to serve clients, or engage with new ones? There's a lot of creative brainpower within you and around you. Start tapping into it.

2. Think like a beginner. Eyeglass maker and creative juggernaut Warby Parker encourages employees to approach the world with a beginner's mindset as a way to embrace curiosity and enhance creativity. This idea, inspired by Buddhist principles, is that while companies are made up of groups of experts who have solutions to problems at their fingertips, sometimes it's better to think like a beginner who has questions that may lead to better, newer solutions. Lawyers spend their careers working toward expert status, but adopting a "beginner" mindset can bring a fresh perspective to one's practice.

Just because you've always billed by the hour, sent a card to your clients during the holidays and published that quarterly newsletter, it doesn't mean it's a good idea to do so in the future. One of the best ways to find out what clients want is to ask them. Experts often think they have all the answers. Beginners like to ask lots of questions. Think like a beginner once in a while.

3. Connect the dots and trust your gut. Creative problem solving doesn't always happen instantly, like a bolt of lightning. Those yellow squares all over your desk prove it. In 1968, a chemist for 3M accidentally developed a weak adhesive that retained its stickiness but had a "removability characteristic."

"We really need to stop considering thinking as simply 'intelligence in action' and think of it as a skill that can be developed by everyone."
— Edward de Bono, 1982

The breakthrough languished for years, with no practical application and little enthusiasm within the company. One idea that was pushed was using the adhesive to create a sticky bulletin board, but it was rejected because there wasn't a big enough bulletin board market to justify the investment. It wasn't until 1974 that a colleague approached the chemist and talked to him about the "aha moment" he had at church while struggling with bookmarks that kept falling out of his hymnbooks. The Post-It was born.

Creative inspiration can come from anywhere, and often when you least expect it. By opening yourself up to new ideas, you can spark your creative potential. Yes, you'll likely encounter lots of naysayers. But almost every great idea was met with resistance at first. A big part of embracing your creativity is trusting your instincts and having the courage to persevere when confronted with doubt.

4. Adapt and embrace your creative side. The legal industry is changing, like it or not. To stay relevant, you need to think differently and act strategically. There is a time and a place for "serious and same" in the practice of law, but marketing and business development is not one of them.

MAKE A CHOICE AND ACT: THE POWER OF INTENTIONALITY

There's a tricky balance that lawyers need to strike: staying focused on the "task at hand" while keeping an eye on the future. The task at hand involves acquiring technical *skills*, such as drafting, negotiation and deposition taking, as well as less tangible but equally important *qualities*, such as judgment, at a relatively early point in one's career. Without these skills and qualities, nothing else matters. There are a lot of golfers that can smack 300-yard drives, but if they can't chip and putt, they're destined for amateur status.

The same principle applies in the legal world. If you want to grow and be successful, there's nothing you can do to get around the prerequisite of becoming a competent practitioner. You need to get a good handle on the fundamentals. But it's harder to know what to do about the future, primarily because it always comes quicker than you think. Ten years out seems like forever, until it's been 15 and you're asking where the time went.

The Future Is Hard Because It's Less Charted

Starting a legal career is the end of the well-lit path of youth for many. Graduate high school, go to college, take the LSAT, attend law school, get a job, pass the bar exam. When we're young there's a process that must be followed, and lawyers like processes. But then what? Work hard and make partner? OK, fine. But that's like saying the Sahara Desert is the way to get from the Atlantic Ocean to the Indian Ocean. It will get you there, but it's going to be a pretty rough ride.

While there are many different paths one can take in a career — some leading to happiness and satisfaction — there's one common denominator that often leads to career misery: loss of control. If your time, and your career path, is dictated by the proclivities and preferences of others, it's hard to get excited about your job.

From Resolution to Action

All of us want things. Every year many of us resolve to make changes — personally and professionally — in order to get what we want. Eat better, write that article, exercise, make those phone calls, spend more time with family, and learn that new skill. But inevitably another year passes without the results we desire and we are back to square one.

For most, the problem is not one of indecision, but one of inaction. The desire for change is strong, but the will to make sustainable change happen is lacking. For this reason, many lawyers spend their careers on autopilot — attending diligently to client needs and priorities but not their own. Days, weeks and years seem to flash by in a whirlwind of emails, conference calls and court appearances. With demanding clients, bosses and adversaries to deal with on a daily basis, who has time to focus on much else?

That's not to say that most lawyers are mindless or aimless about their future. Far from it. Most have broad goals for their career. But far fewer take the steps to achieve those goals. Changing the direction of one's career requires more than wishful thinking. It requires intentionality, which brings discipline to decision-making and purpose to action.

When you think and act intentionally, everything you do is geared toward achievement of a specific objective. If you expect change to happen, you can't just show up to work every day, grind it out and expect specific results. If your daily routine involves working hard at the task at hand, it will get you results, but perhaps not of the variety you're looking for. As 19th century author Henry David Thoreau wrote, "It is not enough to be busy. So are the ants. The question is: What are we busy about?"

Routine — unless it's a thoughtful, purposeful, intentional routine intended to achieve a specific goal — is the enemy of progress. When we let thoughtless routine run our lives and careers, we're unable to chart a course and make progress. To break an unproductive routine and establish a productive one, you must commit to small changes that take you in the direction you want to go. Daily intentional action is required.

Making big change happen is a daunting proposition. Indeed, it's often far easier to make radical change happen on a micro-level than it is to make incremental change happen on a macro-level. But constant intentional action can conquer inertia, procrastination and trepidation.

In her co-authored book, *The Progress Principle: Using Small Wins to Ignite Joy, Engagement, and Creativity at Work*, Harvard Business School Professor Teresa Amabile reveals how companies and managers that focus on achieving small, incremental, daily progress have the most productive and motivated workforces. Small wins, in other words, lead to big successes.

You may find yourself in a rut of routine, and desire to act with intentionality and make meaningful change happen in your career, but you do not know where to focus your energy. There's no easy answer to this problem. It requires dogged persistence, and relentless questioning of how our most precious resource — time — is spent.

To take back control you need to first get clear on what you want. Clarity breeds confidence, and confidence begets action. If you can identify what actions produce the greatest results, then you'll be in a position to focus more of your energy on the most productive tasks.

Hopes and wants do not work as career planning. Intentional action toward an objective that excites you is the path of progress. We are unconsciously forming habits and routines every day. Winning is a habit. So is losing. Why not grab the reins and chart the course you want to be on? Taking back control starts with a choice — a choice that often involves eliminating unproductive activities more than it does adding productive ones. So make a decision to act ... and then act!

PART TWO

BECOMING AN EXPERT

4

THE EXPERTISE EFFECT: HOW GETTING NARROW CAN GROW YOUR PRACTICE

The first phase in any lawyer's career involves building basic competence. Nothing else really matters until you've developed good judgment, effective communication skills and a high — if not yet expert — level of skill in your chosen area of practice.

But then what? There was a time when simply "doing good work" was enough for lawyers to advance in their careers. Clients were institutional, and business development expectations were much different. In today's legal marketplace lawyers must build a book of business.

Having clients is important for several reasons. At many firms it's a require-ment to make partner. It often increases one's compensation. But perhaps, most importantly, it's empowering. Having clients allows a lawyer to have greater control over his career and personal life. Not only is a lawyer with clients a valued asset in her own firm, but she is valuable to others as well.

That's not to say that having clients melts stress away, as it creates a whole new level of responsibility. When you own the client relationship, you own the ultimate responsibility to maintain the relationship.

But in a choice between two alternatives — to have, or not to have, a book of business — the former gives you more options. One of the most unenvi-able positions a lawyer who desires control can be in is to be dependent on others for billable hours. Without clients, a lawyer's time and compensation is reliant upon, and subject to the whims of, his colleagues who have their own books of business.

So how do you take control back? Instead of simply being a lawyer, focus on building a practice. If you have your own clients, you have more control over your career destiny.

When it comes to business development, quality work and technical proficiency are table stakes. Acquiring the skills necessary to develop and sustain a solid client base is required, and that's a much different skill set. In today's market, in which clients are looking for specialists, not generalists, developing business requires niche expertise. While the ethical rules may prevent you from identifying yourself as an "expert" in your particular field(s) of practice, you should be doing everything possible — professionally and authentically — to create this impression in the minds of others.

Time to Take Stock

So how do you know if you're building a practice, rather than simply being a lawyer? Some introspection is required.

- Do you have a long-term plan in place to establish and project expertise in a narrow industry, or are you simply reacting to opportunities as they arise?

- Are you "in the middle" of your target industry, writing and speaking frequently, or are you dabbling in a range of industries?

- Are you genuinely interested and excited about your target industry, or does it simply present an opportunity?

- Do you have a deep understanding of the business issues, or simply the legal ones, that impact your target industry?

- Are new clients seeking you out, or are you seeking out new clients?

- Are you "too busy" to project thought leadership by speaking and writing, or do you prioritize time for these essential activities?

- Are your clients geographically diverse, or are they concentrated in geographic proximity to you?

- Do you solve vexing problems for clients, or do you simply complete assignments for them?

- Is your day structured with activities and initiatives that advance your expert standing, or is it driven by the day's email traffic?

- Do you carefully consider, vet, and often turn away opportunities that aren't the right fit, or do you jump on any new opportunity that presents itself?

- Are your billings and collections steadily climbing, or are they erratic — up one year, down the next?

- Can you perform routine tasks within your niche with little thought and effort, or do matters routinely require you to brush up on the relevant law and industry at issue?

- Do you feel in control of your life, or does your life feel controlled by others?

It doesn't require an expert in business development to tell you which of these are characteristics and behaviors of expert lawyers. But in business, as in life, there's often a big gap between the knowledge we obtain and the actions we take.

We generally *know* what we should be doing. What's missing is the discipline and courage to do what we should be doing. The longer one waits to do, the easier it is to do nothing. So it's important to begin early in one's career. And it won't happen by accident. Many years of dogged, disciplined effort are necessary.

The first step in building a practice and becoming a one-of-a-kind lawyer, then, is establishing expertise in a narrow practice or specialized industry.

Why Get Narrow?

There are countless ways lawyers can and do compete with one another for work. There is price (what work costs); process (how work is performed); personality (the lawyer's and her firm's); place (one's geographic location); and principles ("honesty," "integrity," "work ethic"). These and many others are all characteristics that lawyers emphasize in an effort to differentiate themselves.

But these are not the cards with which you want to play. Expertise in a narrow domain is what good clients crave and are willing to pay a premium for.

Visualize a continuum. On one end is the general practitioner — the "Jack of All Trades" — and on the other is the specialist — the "Master Craftsman."

The Jack of All Trades is busy, bouncing from project to project, learning a little about a lot. Clients think of the Jack of All Trades when price is a primary consideration.

The Jack of All Trades is reactive to opportunities. A client contacts him to handle a family law matter, and he takes it on despite having little prior experience in this area. He spends a great deal of time getting up to speed on family law issues, navigates his way through the engagement, and then decides that he'd like to pursue more work in this area. So he adds a new service area to his website, and adds a new element to his elevator pitch. But then an estate planning matter comes in, and he changes his focus again. And so on. It's difficult, if not impossible, for a lawyer to gain traction if he keeps shifting gears.

The Master Craftsman is also busy, but focused. She knows a lot about a little and is able to charge a price premium. Referral sources think of her when a particular type of expertise is required — she frequently is on the "short list" when potential clients request a referral from other lawyers. She doesn't need to get up to speed on the issues. In most instances, answering questions and determining a plan of action is instinctive for her.

JACK OF ALL TRADES	MASTER CRAFTSMAN
Gets Price-Sensitive Work	Gets Work When Results, Not Price, Matter
Busy and Scattered	Busy and Focused
Seeks Out Work	Is Sought After
Client in Control of Engagement	Controls the Engagement

VS.

She is also able to quickly validate whether a client is appropriate for her practice. The Master Craftsman turns away much more work than the Jack of All Trades, but the work she does take on aligns with her experience, expertise and interests. Because of her past experience, she can quickly and easily determine how much time a matter will take, allowing her to be more creative in developing alternative fee arrangements, often leading to more profitable engagements. Should she so choose, she can work less and earn more than her Jack of All Trades counterparts who spend a great deal more time both developing and completing new business.

Most lawyers fall somewhere in the middle. They don't try to be all things to all clients, but they like to keep their options open. Just think of how many practice areas and industries most lawyers list on their website bio pages. This tendency is largely driven by the fear of missing out on opportunities due to the misguided notion that the more options you provide to the marketplace, the more opportunities will present themselves to you. However, quality, not quantity, of opportunities is what matters. It's also driven by the desire for variety, to do something different each day. The "shiny new toy" factor. It's exciting to get an email or phone call from a prospect, but it's important to know how and when (quickly in most instances) to say no.

That's because there are consequences of fear, and a downside to variety. The less focused you are, the more commoditized you become.

Jack of
All Trades

Most
Lawyers

Master
Craftsman

The more commoditized you become, the more alternatives there are to engaging your practice. The more alternatives there are, the less pricing power you have. As we all learned in Econ 101, price elasticity is driven by the availability of substitutes in a market. The more alternatives, the lower the price, and vice versa.

By commoditizing yourself, you can insulate yourself from fears of missed opportunities, and indulge desires for variety, but it comes at a price. Are you willing to pay it? Consciously or not, most lawyers do.

Ask yourself a question: Would you prefer to have a high-volume, low-fee practice, or a low-volume, high-fee practice? In other words, would you prefer to work more and earn less, or work less and earn more? The answer seems obvious, but the manner in which most lawyers act contradicts the almost rhetorical nature of the question. The allure of the comfortable middle is strong.

Accordingly, while there is comfort in being a generalist, it is false comfort. When you have a niche specialization, you may lose opportunities that don't fit within it, but when you're a generalist, you'll certainly lose the powerful benefits that redound to legal experts.

The market for legal services is simply too competitive to have "some" expertise or "general" industry knowledge. No longer, when asked by a prospective client why they should do business with you, is it effective to answer that, in effect, "I do pretty much the same thing as my competitor, just better." It's necessary to offer clients something different. But to offer something different, you must act differently.

To become an expert, you must go all in.

THE DANGERS OF "THE CLARITY PARADOX"

t's important to keep in mind that there is no permanence to narrowness. Disciplined lawyers who establish narrow practices are at risk of becoming victims of their own success, and slipping back into the generalist trap. In his excellent book, *Essentialism: The Disciplined Pursuit of Less* (which contains innumerable invaluable lessons for lawyers), Greg McKeown discusses the danger of "the clarity paradox," which he explains has four phases:

Phase 1: When we really have clarity of purpose, it leads to success.

Phase 2: When we have success, it leads to more options and opportunities.

Phase 3: When we have increased options and opportunities, it leads to diffused efforts.

Phase 4: Diffused efforts undermine the very clarity that led to our success in the first place.

(Greg McKeown, *Essentialism: The Disciplined Pursuit of Less*. New York: Crown Business, 2014.)

On his blog, McKeown sums up his point as follows: "Curiously, and overstating the point in order to make it, *success is a catalyst for failure.*"

McKeown points out that Jim Collins, in his book *How the Mighty Fall: And Why Some Companies Never Give In*, argues similarly that one of the reasons companies fail is due to "the undisciplined pursuit of more."

The narrow lawyer is the expert lawyer. Expert lawyers are presented with more opportunities than their generalist counterparts. Unless they are careful and discerning, expert lawyers can fall victim to "the clarity paradox." Dogged discipline is required to stay on the right path.

5

CARVING A PATH: HOW TO ESTABLISH AND SUSTAIN EXPERT STATUS

LeBron James is an expert. Michael Jordan was, too, during his playing days. They are two of the most prolific scorers in NBA history. They're also considered two of the best defensive players to ever play the game. They've won championships, MVP trophies and huge endorsement deals, earning tens of millions in the process. So should you try to become the Jordan or James of the legal game? Maybe, but it's probably going to require setting all else — family, friends, outside interests — aside to pursue the pinnacle. A better role model might be Jodie Meeks.

Never heard of the guy? Well, in 2014, Meeks signed a three-year, $19 million contract with the Detroit Pistons. Unlike Jordan or James, he's not a great all-around player, and was primarily a role player who came off the bench for his previous team, the Los Angeles Lakers. But Meeks excels at a skill that NBA teams crave — he's one of the league's best three-point shooters. And he's ridden his ability to perform a narrow, but critical, task to a huge contract and what will likely be a long, lucrative career. The same is true of most left-handed relief pitchers in baseball, whose job descriptions are typically limited to disposing of left-handed hitters in the middle and late innings of games.

How about an example a little closer to home? The most successful expert witnesses are typically those who have embraced the benefits of niche specialization. To be at the top of his or her game, an antitrust expert, for example, must be an expert in an industry such as energy, and oftentimes possess a subspecialty within the industry. Complex litigation hinges on narrow and often related issues that require different experts to prove or defend against various claims. When much is at stake, a team of experts consisting of individuals with narrow, niche expertise, rather than a single individual with broad expertise, is engaged.

The point is that, in the legal marketplace, to reap the benefits of being an expert you don't need to be the world's foremost litigator or M&A strategist. Those are big ponds with lots of fish swimming in them. Remember, "expert" is a relative term. A better approach is to think narrower. The law is vast and complex, so drill deep, not wide.

For most, potential areas of expertise to pursue can be identified at the intersection of interests, experience and market opportunities. So ask yourself three questions:

1. What type of work do I like to do?

2. What type of work am I good at?

3. What opportunities exist in the marketplace? In other words, are people buying what I'd like to sell?

If you can determine what you like to do, what you're good at and where market opportunities exist, and then find some commonality among them, you will be in good shape when it comes to carving out a niche.

Take, for example, a former colleague of mine. Fairly early in his career he established himself as a skilled corporate bankruptcy lawyer (what he's good at — but a broad, "big pond" area of the law). While his knowledge and experience was in U.S. bankruptcy law, he always had an interest in aspects of international law (what interests him). A career in U.S. bankruptcy law does not necessarily lend itself to opportunities and exposure to international law issues, but that

didn't stop him. He identified opportunities to develop expertise in the narrow, but important, area of how the U.S. Bankruptcy Code and U.K. pension law intersect and impact each other. He honed his expertise in this area before the 2008 financial crisis and restructuring wave, and when the wave hit (the market opportunity) he was well positioned for important engagements in U.S. bankruptcy cases that involved these international issues.

Pursuing what interests you is probably the most important predictor of, if not success, satisfaction. And success typically follows satisfaction.

Psychologist and Yale School of Management professor Amy Wrzesniewski focuses her work on how people make meaning of their work, and the experiences of those who perceive their work as a job, career or calling. Her findings reveal that those who view their work as a "job" derive little meaning and see it only as a means (income) to an end (buying life's necessities). If given the opportunity, they would start doing other work immediately if it led to greater income. Those who view their work as a "career" are more satisfied and engaged, but still desire more — more compensation, benefits and responsibility. Those who view their work as a "calling" are most satisfied. To them, work is not a means to an end, but a source of joy, meaning and fulfillment.

Wrzesniewski's work holds important lessons for aspiring lawyer-experts. Few, if any, lawyers who view their work as a job will achieve expert status. Someone who goes through the motions, punches the clock and has his or her eye on an exit strategy is extremely unlikely to put in the essential hard work. A lawyer engaged in a career can become an expert through sheer will and ambition. But if the work does not inspire him or her, it will be difficult to sustain expert status during the course of a long career with dogged persistence alone.

But a lawyer who is pursuing his calling, whose work is stimulating and satisfying, will become an expert almost despite himself. He thinks about his work off the clock, not because he has to, but because he wants to. He believes that his work adds value to the lives of others. This enables him to learn and think creatively about his subject matter in ways that others don't, or even can't.

Wrzesniewski suggests that those who view their work as a job, or even a career, engage in an exercise called "job crafting." She and her colleagues describe job crafting as "redefining your job to incorporate your motives, strengths and passions. The exercise prompts you to visualize the job, map its elements, and reorganize them to better suit you." In other words, job crafting involves taking intentional action to take control of your career (and hopefully transform it into a calling).

A good place to start? Determine: (1) if you like doing something and (2) if you're good at it. If both are true, and there's a market that exists for the type of service you intend to provide, you may have found your niche.

CREATE A CATEGORY OF ONE

What happens when you figure out the niche you want to pursue, but then determine that no one else is providing the service? To some, that's grounds for fear and anxiety. Many lawyers, after learning that no one else is doing what they are proposing to do, would draw the conclusion that their idea lacks merit. After all, if there was a market for their niche, surely someone else would have beat them to it, right?

To others, though, this scenario is grounds for optimism. Businesses, particularly in the tech sector, strive to be in a "category of one." Books have been written extolling the virtues of companies such as Google, Facebook, LinkedIn and Starbucks that occupy this hallowed ground. But lawyers and law firms tend to be a conservative bunch, and have a hard time breaking free from the pack.

Daniel O'Rielly and Dena Roche are two lawyers who made the leap. After successful stints as associates with top-tier firms, both large and small, they decided to hang their own shingle and formed the law firm O'Rielly & Roche LLP. As litigators, and as is typical of most lawyers starting out on their own, they took on much of what came in the door. With considerable experience as trial lawyers and in complex business litigation, including representing financial institutions in consumer finance litigation, a significant percentage of their work and their business development activity was focused in this area.

It was good work for big clients, particularly for two young lawyers out on their own. It provided consistent cash flow. It felt safe.

But as Dan and Dena, and their firm, matured and grew as legal service providers, they began thinking bigger and more strategically about their practice. They had the opportunity to work on matters for clients they had never served before — other lawyers and law firms — helping them to navigate the business, legal and ethical issues that arise when law firm partners depart and transition to new firms.

After several years working on such matters, Dan and Dena determined that they liked doing this type of work. They enjoyed playing the role of strategic counsel to sophisticated clients, and the fact that while their strong litigation backgrounds were assets that clients valued, the work itself was not primarily litigation oriented.

They also found that, while other lawyers did this type of work, few if any did so exclusively. There wasn't even really an existing practice area, at least being marketed in California where their firm is based, that captured the service that they were providing.

So what did they do? They created a "category of one" practice area called "Partner Departure Law." They began promoting the service on their website, and writing about the topic on their blog, California Partner Departure Law (www.partnerdeparturelaw.com). And the work started flowing in — interesting, profitable work for sophisticated clients. They knew they were on to something.

Rather than playing it safe and marketing this niche as part of a broader litigation practice, they rebranded and re-oriented their firm to focus on partner departure issues. Litigation is a component of that practice, but their target audience — lawyers and law firms — is clearly defined. Because they are niched, their content marketing efforts (the primary method of marketing their practice) are more effective. Having seen the fruits of their labor with their blog focused on partner departure issues, they started a second blog, California Attorney Ethics Counsel (www.attorneyethicscounsel.com), targeting the same audience, but addressing more specifically the ethical issues that lawyers and firms face.

As Dan and Dena found, creating a category of one in the legal marketplace is not easy, but it's an effort worth making.

Building Blocks of the Expert Lawyer

Being an expert is rewarding. Experts make more money. The work experts do is often more interesting, too. Work that a generalist may find demanding in a particular area of the law, requiring a review of case law, statutes and court rules, is routine for an expert. That which requires thought and research invites equivocation and uncertainty, while that which is routine is trained reflex, done with confidence and clarity. As a result, an expert's mind is unshackled to think more deeply, examine problems differently and find solutions that generalists often cannot. This makes for a more interesting, enjoyable career.

Of course, these rewards are not free. Once an expert, not always an expert. Sustaining a market-leading position requires hard work, continuing education, forward thinking and creativity. Here are a few tips:

- **Learn and do.** True expertise comes from acquiring both knowledge and experience. You need to find time for both book learning and real-world experience. Because experts take a narrow approach to their practice, they are able to immerse themselves in industries in which they focus — reading, writing and attending events focused on the same issues that their clients care about. This allows them not only to have legal subject matter expertise, but also, more importantly, expertise about the business issues impacting their clients.

- **Be a thought leader.** Content marketing — real thought leadership expressed in the marketplace of ideas — is an essential element of establishing and sustaining expertise. Not only will you promote your credentials, but the act of writing will force you to become more informed about your area of expertise.

- **Be disciplined.** The road to expertise (one that never really ends) is filled with distractions. Start small, learn your craft, and don't get derailed by new "opportunities" that can slow your progression. As a result, you'll end up saying "no" quite often — perhaps more than you say "yes" — but that's not a sign of failure. It's a sign of attaining confident expert status.

- **Get a mentor.** Just as Michael Jordan had a coach, experts rely on others that help them excel. Professional colleagues, mentors, business coaches — whoever you trust and respect — can often provide helpful feedback, perspective, reassurance and advice. Perhaps most importantly, a trusted sounding board can help hold you accountable if you get off track. An outside perspective is often needed, even for the most committed and accomplished experts in any field.

- **Be confident and take risks.** No one else will think you are an expert if you don't think of yourself as one. Fear of failure is one of the biggest challenges you'll face. Being an expert involves, first and foremost, taking ownership and responsibility. Experts don't outsource and equivocate, they are confident and decisive. You have to be willing to take chances to learn and grow.

The world does not need more general practitioners. What is needed, and what good clients are willing to pay a premium for, is deep knowledge and expertise in narrow practices and industries. While being a generalist may make you relevant to all, being an expert makes you indispensable to some. Be indispensable.

SOME QUESTIONS TO ASK YOURSELF

1. What type of work do you enjoy doing?

2. Do you have experience doing the work you enjoy for clients in a growing industry?

3. Are you genuinely interested in learning more about the legal and business issues concerning a particular industry?

4. Are there mentors within your firm who you can model yourself after?

5. Can you leverage your past experience to bring new perspectives to a new industry?

6. Can you quickly and easily answer questions, and provide advice, on basic issues in your area of purported expertise?

7. What are three trends that are transforming the industry you serve? Are there any legal solutions that can help clients overcome the challenges, or seize the opportunities, that these trends present?

8. What legal issues and questions are you passionate and interested in?

9. What insights could clients and prospective clients benefit from?

10. How can you learn and/or validate what those insights are?

AN EXPERT PROFILE

Scott Becker is a Harvard Law School graduate and chair of McGuireWoods' healthcare practice. Early on in his career, as a mid-level associate, he realized that to get control over his life, and direction over his career, he needed to build a practice. He became "intent on building something."

He began by taking a look around him to see how other lawyers in his firm that he admired and respected — and who had built practices themselves — went about the process. He discovered commonalities and found a mentor who was willing to help.

His mentor, also a healthcare lawyer, urged him to carve out a niche for himself. Scott realized that having a niche would mean working with clients with similar problems, and he would be able to build up his expertise in that area and offer it to those similarly situated.

He began by experimenting. According to Scott, "There is no perfect plan, you need to experiment to figure out what works."

However, as a young lawyer, Scott realized that achieving expert status and building a practice really was the long game. "You can't aim straight for the top. It's almost impossible to compete with big firms who are putting huge resources into protecting their biggest clients. But there are lots of smaller clients in niche industries that you can pursue. As you build up your practice and your expertise, then later in your career you'll be in a position to go after the bigger clients. You need to hit singles and doubles before you can hit home runs."

With the support of his firm, he identified three potential niche areas within the healthcare industry that were underserved but had potential and began pursuing that work. He drew upon the principles of a business book he read early in his career that emphasized the importance of "getting in the middle" of the industry you are focused on. Heeding that lesson, he created newsletters geared toward each niche and began hosting small industry conferences. He gained traction with one — surgical centers — and poured all of his energy into it.

Once his direction was clear, he created an action plan to develop business. He was intent on building a practice, but didn't want to be the guy that was trying to sell to his friends and family. "If I was going to be in it for the long haul, I knew I needed to create a marketing and business development platform that was going to be sustainable and reach more broadly than my inner circle," Scott said.

Scott realized that if he wanted to build a sustainable practice, he needed to get himself, and his expertise, in front of as many potential clients as frequently as possible. He focused his efforts on creating and disseminating useful information to industry leaders. In other words, he focused on content marketing, before that term became part of the marketing lexicon.

His newsletter became widely read, and he became widely known. And he began to develop business — lots of it. After he became known as an expert in his surgical centers niche, larger opportunities with hospitals and healthcare systems began presenting themselves.

But he never stopped doing what got him there — staying in the middle of the industry he was focused on. What started as a newsletter grew into one of the most widely read, and most widely respected, healthcare publishing platforms in the world. Becker's Healthcare now publishes a portfolio of five industry-leading trade publications and is a successful business itself. It's also a big part of what drives Scott's successful legal practice.

To what does Scott attribute his success? Picking a niche and sticking with it. "It takes a tremendous amount of effort. You need to constantly be in front of your audience providing personalized content."

Scott believes that the biggest problem most people have is lack of commitment. "Most lawyers don't get results quickly enough so they don't stick with it. Building a practice is a serious job — a full-time job — and you need to treat it as such."

PART THREE

BRANDING YOURSELF AS AN EXPERT

6

SUBSTANCE AND FORM: ELEMENTS OF A LAWYER BRAND

Branding. It's one of the most overworked and overanalyzed topics in the marketplace of ideas. Paradoxically, or perhaps consequently, it's also one of the most misunderstood. This misunderstanding isn't a definitional one. There's a general consensus that a brand "is the sum of what others think of you," or something similar. But there are two pertinent, preliminary questions beyond "what is branding?" worthy of exploration: Why is it important? And how is it done?

Reputation and Brand — A Distinction Without a Difference?

Most of the discussion in the legal industry focuses on law firm branding. But it's important to realize that while your firm has a brand, you do too. Unless you're the boss, you may have little control over how your firm is positioned. But you're in control of your personal brand.

Some balk at the term "personal branding" and argue that it's a clumsy, meaningless substitute for "reputation." But there's a difference.

A lawyer's reputation is a critical component of her personal brand, but the terms aren't synonymous. Branding requires a concerted, strategic and active effort to describe, position and promote how one's skills and expertise are relevant and uniquely able to solve a client's problems. It's not just about letting your reputation speak for itself. It's purposefully injecting your unique value proposition into the marketplace. While reputation is something that happens to you, brand is something you make happen. Developing your personal brand, therefore, is critical to promoting your expert status.

Ever wonder why the guy down the street with similar skills, experience, pricing and reputation consistently scores more opportunities than you? It very well may be that he focuses time and energy on developing and promoting his personal brand such that he is top of mind when clients need help of the variety he provides. You may be just as equipped to provide the help, but you don't get the call because you take a more passive approach to promoting yourself. You rely on your reputation, when you should be building your brand. Active, strategic management — that's the critical difference between your reputation and your brand.

Why? Your Positive Mark

The market for legal services is fiercely competitive and lawyers need every edge they can get. A compelling brand can provide one. The previous section of this book focused on the importance of establishing expertise to build an interesting, profitable practice. That's step one.

Step two is learning how to package, position and promote that expertise to the marketplace. To stand out, a lawyer must be mindful of both substance (expertise) and form (brand).

Think about how many times you've been asked what you do for a living, or what practice area you're in, and eyes have glazed over at your answer. How many pitches have you been involved in where you begin describing your background and your audience's attention drifts toward email? How many people actually read from start to finish, let alone engage with, your firm's website bio or LinkedIn page?

Do you leave a positive impression, a memorable mark, after any of these interactions? If not, why not?

Developing your personal brand doesn't mean being boastful. A well-defined and developed brand simply lets people know who you are and what you're good at. They'll know your strengths, the value you provide and the types of situations you're uniquely qualified to assist with. Accordingly, once you've clearly defined what you do and for whom, you won't have to chase as much business — it will start chasing you.

You'll also have more leverage to charge a premium. Think about your own past experience hiring a service provider to handle an important issue for you. Before committing to someone, you probably felt a certain level of unease. Does this person know what he is doing? Is the price fair? Will he do what he says?

Anxiety is heightened by vague claims and meaningless platitudes communicated by the service provider. On the other hand, a calm description of expertise, experience and confidence in addressing the problem increases your own confidence that you are speaking to the right person. You focus less on price than you would if you still felt uncomfortable about the person's abilities. After all, you likely care more about outcome than price — the very essence of value — and you're willing to pay a bit more if you trust that the problem will be addressed the first time, without having to go through the process again.

Conversely, a poorly defined and developed brand will leave your market confused about, or unaware altogether of, you and your practice.

HOW TO DEVELOP YOUR PERSONAL BRAND

Personal brands aren't created; they're developed. It's a subtle point, but not a pedantic one. "Creating" a brand suggests that branding is a one-time or short-term event, when it's really a process — a lifelong one. Brands evolve over time, just as you do.

There's no single path or method to create a compelling personal brand, so I won't suggest one. Sometimes blueprint methods work well, but in an endeavor such as this that is intensely personal and requires big, bold thinking, there is no single blueprint to follow.

But there are benchmarks. For a personal brand to be effective, it must be authentic, unique and bold. And it must grow and progress as you do in your life and career.

Authentic

People crave authenticity and transparency, and nothing is more authentic or transparent than being yourself, warts and all. Don't try to be someone you are not — your brand will suffer for it, and it's unsustainable. As Anne Morrow Lindbergh once said, "The most exhausting thing you can do is to be is inauthentic."

One of the best ways to be authentic is to tell your story, as opposed to reciting your resume. From client pitches, to website bios, to social media engagement, expressing your brand as a story will help build something people care about, can relate to and want to buy into. People connect with stories because they are memorable and evoke emotion — that's why lawyers are taught to craft a story through their closing arguments and brief writing.

Consider the following possible responses by a young lawyer to the dreaded "Tell me about yourself?" question in a social business setting:

LAWYER A:

"I graduated from the University of Michigan Law School and specialize in corporate bankruptcy law."

LAWYER B:

"I was a junior in college when I realized how little journalism graduates earn out of school, so I rushed to apply to law school, knowing nothing about the practice of law. I got accepted into a mid-tier school, loved the challenge and curriculum, worked my tail off, transferred to and graduated from the University of Michigan. After graduation, I was supposed to be an M&A lawyer, but my first day of work was on Monday, September 17, 2001, and virtually every new associate in the firm was tossed into the bankruptcy department given the economic impact of 9/11. It was intense, terrifying, challenging and exhilarating."

The first is the response I typically gave when I practiced — while true, it's utterly forgettable. The second is more along the lines of what I should have said — it's more authentic and memorable, and would have helped shape my brand story at that point in my career.

Storytelling allows you to frame your uniqueness and connect the dots between the client's needs and the value you provide. It creates loyalty and bonds with clients and colleagues. That's because in relationships — attorney/client ones included — people crave authenticity and inspiration. A good brand story can deliver both.

Bold

Your brand story should be more manifesto than bio. Your narrative should describe not just where you are in your life and career, but where you want to go. It should be aspirational. Think of it as goal setting. By being bold you'll not only stake out new ground for yourself, but you'll create some personal accountability, too. Your career objective is no longer an abstract in your mind, but a crucial element of your brand story.

Unique

Large full-service firms that are structured similarly offer similar services and serve similar markets and industries, have difficulty — with good reason — developing a brand that convinces audiences they are different in any meaningful sense. That's not to say it's impossible, or that some don't do it extremely well, but it's hard. A narrowly focused expert, on the other hand, can move past generalities, hyperbole and embellishments and develop a brand that draws notice. You're an original — your brand should be also. Therefore, a unique personal brand is developed not simply by defining who you are, but just as importantly by defining who you are not.

In this context, being unique is also as dependent on how you act as it is about what you say. In an industry that is largely conservative, conformist and commoditized, individual attorneys have an outstanding opportunity to develop a unique brand based on the client experiences they create, as opposed to the things they say about themselves. From pricing to hospitality, communication to education, there are countless ways lawyers can create unique, valuable experiences for clients that can set them apart.

With a few simple steps, you can take control of your personal brand.

Listen. Listen to what others say about you. This may seem obvious, but much can be learned about what others think about you by listening closely to how they introduce you to others at business meetings, cocktail parties and networking events. Is their description about you and your practice compelling, or even accurate?

Conduct a Digital Audit. Ever "Googled" yourself to see where you pop up online? Take it one step further by auditing not just where you show up, but what is being said about you. This includes information on platforms that you control such as LinkedIn and your website bio, as well information on those you don't control, like Avvo and Yelp.

Strategize and Seize Control. Once you have a sense of what your brand is — that is, the perception others currently have of you — it's easier to develop a strategy to take control of and build the brand you want. Start by turning off the distractions, grabbing a pen and notepad, and writing down the characteristics and values that you'd like to be known for (keeping in mind the need to be authentic). From this exercise, develop and write down a short professional manifesto or mantra.

In corporate branding this is often referred to as the brand positioning statement — a brief, powerful encapsulation of a business's values, aspirations and key points of differentiation. This positioning statement becomes a cornerstone and touch point for all corporate messaging and marketing activity.

Similarly, by developing a personal brand positioning statement, and then refining how you think, speak, write and otherwise communicate about yourself (offline and online), you can help to ensure that the way others think about you is more consistent with how you want to be thought of.

Practice. It's a misnomer that only extroverts who thrive in the public spotlight can have dynamic personal brands. Many introverts have cultivated powerful brand names. But introverts and extroverts alike must practice their professional pitch in order to build their personal brand. This may involve taking a writing or public speaking course. For almost everyone it means being mindful of and practicing the message you want to convey to others before meeting new people at networking events and other potential relationship-building forums. Building a personal brand takes practice.

The Transformative Power of the Digital Age

In today's digital age, it's more important than ever to manage one's personal brand. Before social media, a personal brand could largely be contained. If you didn't put yourself "out there" by networking aggressively, advertising, speaking, writing and pursuing public relations opportunities, the market's awareness of your brand resulted and spread primarily due to word of mouth.

Today, whether you like it or not, your brand is out there. People search for you on LinkedIn. Your Avvo profile is available. Your firm's website bio is often the first impression you make. Former clients may have reviewed you on Yelp. It's imperative, therefore, to embrace and leverage social media platforms to publish ideas of your own, and share those of others, to help others to understand your story, your interests and your areas of expertise.

If you're not actively crafting the personal brand that you want to exist online, there's a pretty good chance that one you don't is already there.

Is It Working?

Let's say you've bought into the benefits of developing your brand, and have been actively and strategically managing your brand for six months or more. You've narrowed your focus, begun presenting yourself differently and more purposefully with clients and prospective clients, improved your Internet and social media presence, put your thought leadership in the public domain, and generally sharpened your brand in line with your expertise. What are some signs you should look for to know whether your efforts are paying off?

1. Peers. Other attorneys and professionals will have taken notice, and better understand what you do. As a result, you'll receive more referrals that are in line with your expertise, and fewer that are not.

2. Clients, too. As with referral sources, clients and prospective clients will have a better idea of where your expertise lies. They'll know what you do and how you can help, and new opportunities will reflect that understanding.

3. You'll be more visible. Because you are a more focused and visible expert in your niche, both online and offline, your content marketing and speaking efforts have likely become sharper and more beneficial. Your ideas are attracting more ears and eyeballs and, consequently, new opportunities to speak and write present themselves.

4. You'll be more profitable. One of the key factors that drives down prices is the availability of substitutes. As a well-branded expert you'll be able to charge more.

5. You'll be more productive. Once you narrow your focus, and focus your energy, you'll increase productivity. You'll feel less scattered because you'll no longer be trying to serve and please everyone.

6. At a minimum, you'll be more purposeful. Many of us approach our careers without a plan and drift from day to day, then year to year. Before you know it, you're in a rut that you can't get out of. By focusing on developing a personal brand that is authentic, bold and unique, you'll have something to aspire to, and benchmark against, on a consistent basis.

No Hiding

More than ever — through the reach of the Internet, social media and business networking sites, and the plethora of publishing and advertising outlets available — you have the power to craft your own unique brand story. At the same time, if you don't take control of your brand, you can't hide from it. Your uninspiring story is still out there for all to see.

Your brand, just as your reputation, develops every day — for better or for worse. So there's no time like the present to start working on yours.

SOME QUESTIONS TO ASK YOURSELF

1. What do you truly want to be known for?

2. What can you do better than anyone else?

3. What problems do others seek you out to solve?

4. How do friends and colleagues describe you to other people?

5. What excites you? What are your passions?

6. What are your core values?

7. Where do you see yourself in five years?

8. When is the last time you've thought about your "elevator pitch"?

9. How often do you update your social media profiles?

10. Do you consistently review how your competitors are positioning themselves in the marketplace?

8

TURN CLIENTS INTO CLIENT-ADVOCATES: THE BRAND EXPERIENCE

Research suggests that life experiences, not material things, are the key to happiness. Nonetheless, by and large people still choose to spend more of their money on material items because they believe they're of greater value. After all, it's pretty easy to peg a value to a new flat-screen TV that costs $3,000. But it's hard to estimate the value of a great memory born of an amazing experience.

The same principle applies in marketing. Provide a service to a client and you'll earn a fee. But provide a positive, memorable experience and you'll earn not just a fee, but a loyal ally and enthusiastic advocate for your firm. Clients will come back for more — and bring others with them.

What Is Brand Experience?

There are two types of services that lawyers can provide to clients. The first is legal service, which relates to quality of professional skill and work product. Legal service is, obviously, critically important to the success of a client relationship. But let's face it, most clients cannot distinguish between good and great work product. Moreover, basic competence and technical proficiency are often presumed — table stakes when it comes to business development opportunities.

The second type of service lawyers provide is client service, which relates to the quality of brand experience one creates. The previous chapter focused on the importance of building a personal brand, which involves telling clients and prospective clients what to think about you. But that is only half of the brand equation. Equal, if not more, attention must be focused on creating an authentic brand experience, where your brand speaks for itself through its interaction with clients.

So what does this mean in the real world? While many clients cannot judge for themselves the quality of legal work product, all clients can distinguish between an attorney who returns calls and responds to emails in a timely fashion and another who doesn't; one who writes clearly, and another whose communication is filled with jargon and legalese; one whose receptionist is pleasant and reception area is aesthetically pleasing, and another whose staff is rude and workspace is cluttered; and one who proactively counsels, educates and imparts wisdom, and another who is always reactive.

Brand experience is about providing intangible value that leads to tangible results. From the start of a pitch, to the conclusion of a matter, to the interim period between engagements, lawyers need to create experiences that make clients want more. Pleasant, educational, professional, and interesting experiences are fundamental to building a one-of-a-kind practice.

Brand messaging can be knocked off — that's a big reason why most firms look and sound so similar. But unique, authentic brand experiences cannot.

It's About Understanding Your Clients' Feelings, Motivations and Desires

As lawyers, we don't like to talk about feelings very much. We are rational, logical problem solvers, and feelings don't really help us get to the right answer when facing a complex legal question. But feelings and emotions — not necessarily logic or rationality — drive many consumer-buying decisions, even important ones like the purchase of sophisticated legal services. Lawyers don't necessarily need to embrace this truth, but they ignore it at their own peril.

Ask a client why they chose one lawyer over another, and you'll often learn that it just "felt" like the right fit. It's for the same reason that a new client becomes a long-term client (again, assuming quality work product). In other words, the client likes the attorney and the experience of working with him or her. The fact that the lawyer "wins" every time often is a secondary consideration.

Where do these positive feelings derive from? A client who feels that he is treated with respect, that his time and opinions are valued, and that his lawyer is invested in his matter is likely to be a satisfied client. But writing the best legal brief, or drawing up the most creative, bullet-proof contract, will never engender this sense of loyalty. It can only happen by creating a positive experience, not just a positive outcome. Brand experience, therefore, is making clients feel good while delivering on your brand promise.

The Ritz-Carlton gets it. Sure, The Ritz-Carlton has beautiful properties in great locations. But so do many other hotel and resort brands. What allows The Ritz-Carlton to charge a premium for its rooms? A big part of its success is due to its "credo" in which it states that "The Ritz-Carlton experience enlivens the senses, instills well-being, and fulfills even the unexpressed wishes and needs of our guests."

For many lawyers it is hard enough to meet, let alone exceed, the expressed desires of clients. So how can lawyers take it a step further and, like The Ritz-Carlton, focus on "unexpressed wishes and needs" of the clients they serve?

It all starts with awareness. The Ritz-Carlton urges its employees to always be conscious of guests' unexpressed needs — the phrase it uses to encourage this behavior is "Radar on — Antenna up." Have you walked in your clients' shoes and stress-tested your brand experience recently? If not, you should.

The Six Pillars of Brand Experience

Lawyers and law firms fail to focus on brand experience for various reasons. One is lack of awareness — with everything else on their plates, it's simply not on the radar screen. Another is lack of

SIX PILLARS
OF LAW FIRM BRANDING

The Pitch

Communication

Client Onboarding

Billing Practices

Hospitality

Training & Education

understanding — it's not considered a priority. Perhaps the biggest reason is fear — there's perceived safety and comfort (albeit false) in conformity. But rather than worrying about being different, the focus should be on being better. Being a better lawyer, building a better personal brand and providing a better brand experience.

There are six pillars to creating an awesome brand experience.

1. The Pitch. When forming new client relationships, it all starts, and too often ends, with the pitch. Instead of reciting bios and reading PowerPoint slides, use the stage you've been provided to add some theatrics to what's typically a pedestrian performance. Dig into the details of the challenges faced by the prospective client to demonstrate not just a sense of who you are, but what it would be like to work with you.

Do your homework in advance and impart some wisdom by educating the client about industry trends, risks they may face from recent rules and regulations, and unconsidered opportunities.

Want to really stand out? Instead of speaking in generalities, ask the prospective client to be specific about current challenges and opportunities, then provide some specific solutions to address them. Sure, you'll be "giving away" your intellectual capital ... but so what? In most cases the client is not interviewing lawyers because he wants free advice. He's looking for someone smart who is not only able to come up with a solution, but implement it as well. By instilling confidence that you have a good handle on the specific issues at hand, you will help the client overcome a big hurdle — which is comfort that you are not just a knowledgeable, competent lawyer, but that you are a knowledgeable, competent lawyer equipped to handle the client's unique issues.

Finally, when meeting with a prospective client, focus on "receiving" rather than "pitching," and ask more questions than you answer. We all hate being sold to, but most of us enjoy talking about ourselves. Being a good listener allows you to understand what really matters to the new client, and not what you think matters.

2. Client onboarding. For many lawyers and law firms, "onboarding" a client involves an exchange of signatures on an engagement letter full of legalese dealing with things like "mandatory arbitration" and "forum selection." Not only is this unpleasant for clients, it's a missed opportunity for lawyers. Onboarding — how a client is welcomed into a firm — should be a process that puts the client at ease, rather than causing the client to put his or her guard up.

By focusing on onboarding, a lawyer can provide an efficient, effective and differentiated client service and brand experience. Onboarding should be a discovery process during which you get to know your client and the client gets to know you. A great way to do this is to provide clients with a written set of principles, promises and processes that explain the brand experience you offer. By getting it out there in writing, you and your staff will be more apt to live up to it.

Onboarding is a time for setting expectations, and addressing questions and concerns from the outset. Halfway through the engagement is not the time to find out you had different expectations about objectives or pricing. Having those conversations up-front will preempt an uncomfortable one down the road.

It's hard to exceed a client's expectations when it comes to the legal services you provide. After all, many legal matters result in all parties walking away with some level of dissatisfaction — that's just the nature of the business. But one area that you can, with relative ease, provide some "wow" factor is developing a dynamic onboarding process that enhances the client's brand experience with you and your firm.

3. Communication. Communication is key to brand experience. Nothing can spoil a relationship quicker than failing to communicate timely and effectively with a client. Effective communication requires three steps: requesting preferences, being proactive and identifying problem solvers.

- Request preferences. During the onboarding process, ask your client his or her preference for receiving information from you. Some like email, some prefer phone calls. Others want to meet face to face. Some appreciate access to updates and information via a cloud-based project management system. Timing is also important. A one-size-fits-all approach of providing biweekly status updates doesn't work for everyone. But you'll never know unless you ask. If you really want to step up your game, try sending a handwritten note once in a while.

- Be proactive. Being reactive, rather than proactive, in your communications is a surefire way to spoil a brand experience. By the time a client reaches out to you for an update, it's likely that she has been wanting one for several days. Conversely, some clients are turned off by too much communication, seeing dollar signs every time an email from you lands in their inbox. This problem is easily avoided, though, by learning the client's preferences up front. That way everyone's expectations are set, and you can tailor your approach accordingly.

- Identify problem solvers. Finally, provide clients with an outlet for communicating concerns. Designate a client ally — someone who can receive and, more importantly, resolve problems or misunderstandings that may arise. Larger firms with more resources may consider hiring a chief experience officer whose sole job is ensuring that clients are well cared for. At smaller firms, the partner in charge of the matter may assume this role. The important thing is that the client has someone to turn to, or else she may turn to another firm.

4. Billing practices. We all know that clients disdain endless series of ".1 hours" and ".2 hours" time entries on bills. But what can be done about billing to better the brand experience? For starters, try to create time entries that explain the value provided, not simply the services provided. Better yet, don't sell time. Declare independence from the timesheet and adopt a value pricing model. While some lawyers and firms have trended in this direction, there's a tremendous amount of room for brand experience innovation here.

Developing a value pricing model is a powerful brand experience tool. It will help with the pitch — you'll stand out. It will help with onboarding — the client will have greater peace of mind knowing that he won't have "bill shock" down the road. And it helps with communication — the client won't be apprehensive about making a phone call for fear of getting charged. By focusing less on inputs (time spent) and more on outputs (value provided), you'll create a better brand experience for your clients.

5. Hospitality. Does visiting your office feel like a trip to the dentist, or to The Ritz-Carlton? Drab decor, rude or unhelpful staff, and lack of basic amenities such as hot coffee and cold water all diminish a client's perception of the value being provided. Hospitality is an area ripe for stress testing. Simply enlist a third-party confidant to call and visit your firm and share his impressions. The feedback will be enlightening.

The need for hospitality is critical to building a good law firm brand experience. Many lawyers forget that while a client's matter may seem routine to them, it's anything but to the client. Most clients, unless they have substantial experience working with lawyers, are nervous when interacting with lawyers and their staff members. They are unfamiliar with the process, wary of the costs and generally unsure of themselves. Lack of hospitality only exacerbates the situation. In the medical field, the brusque, impersonal behavior and demeanor of a doctor and his or her staff is described as "bad bedside manner."

There may not be a name for it in the legal world, but the failure to provide good hospitality and put clients at ease leads to the same bad experience.

6. Training and Education. Clients engage lawyers not just because they are smart, but because they want to get smarter themselves, too. Client training and education, therefore, is a big part of brand experience. Not only is it appreciated by clients, but it's a great way to stay close to clients between matters.

There are countless things you can do, but a good place to start is to host thoughtful events, webinars and education sessions, and generate helpful thought leadership. Set out to help your clients with no expectation of receiving something in return. Call it karma, call it being in the right place at the right time, but it's often when you aren't trying to generate business that good things happen.

Here's a specific idea: Provide lunch and do a training session on location for a client you haven't worked for in a while. I bet you walk away with a new matter.

Bake It into Your Culture

Unless you are a solo practitioner — and I mean "solo," no assistant or paralegal — you'll need to build a brand experience culture in which everyone on your team is invested. The Ritz-Carlton accomplishes this by focusing intensely on training and then baking its customer service principles into its company culture. It starts every day at every property around the world with 15-minute staff meetings at which employees gather to share "wow stories," which are examples of employees going above and beyond to "wow" guests.

Building an outstanding brand experience for your clients requires a similar commitment. It's work, but there will be a great return on investment in terms of client retention, loyalty and satisfaction.

The Value of Brand Experience

The benefits of creating a great brand experience are bountiful.

Business development. Without differentiation, even if a client is not entirely pleased with its current firm, there's little reason to make a switch (the "devil you know" conundrum). A unique, valuable brand experience can provide motivation to make a change. At the very least, you'll be top of mind when the client next gets frustrated by his current firm's lack of brand experience — whether it be rude staff, unreturned phone calls or indecipherable invoices.

Pricing. Clients turn to lawyers when they face challenges or opportunities. In such circumstances, price is less of a factor in purchasing decisions. Just as most consumers don't skimp when it comes to buying an infant car seat, most clients are willing to invest in their lawyer. In other words, clients aren't price sensitive, they're value sensitive.

This statement may strike some as mere claptrap, inconsistent with their own real-world experiences in which they are incessantly beaten down on price by seemingly price-sensitive clients. But those who find themselves in this position must ask themselves a simple question: Am I selling a commodity or providing real value? If you're selling a commodity — meaning the services you provide are largely indistinguishable from those of your competitors — you'll be competing on price.

But clients aren't looking for cheap; in fact, most are suspicious of low-cost service providers. If confronted with no other basis for choosing a lawyer, however, they will opt for the lowest cost. Just as Starbucks and The Ritz-Carlton have created environments in which they can sell a cup of coffee or four walls and a bed at a premium, lawyers must provide clients a similarly unique experience in order to command higher pricing. Value, in the form of an outstanding brand experience, serves as a powerful point of differentiation.

Loyalty. It's much easier to retain an existing client than to find a new one. And for most firms, expanding existing relationships is a leading source of new business. Lawyers and law firms that create great brand experiences create clients for life. Moreover, clients will want to share this experience with others, evolving from being simply clients to being client-advocates.

Think Like Apple

Apple isn't just a technology company. It's a technology company that has revolutionized retail. Customers don't just want Apple's gadgets. They want the unique, interesting and fun experience that Apple offers, primarily through its retail experience. The gadgets — priced at a huge premium — are a means to an end. What makes Apple's disruption of retail so amazing is that the retail industry was, ostensibly, already intensely focused on customer experience. But Apple was still able to upend the industry, creating a category of one that no one has been able to duplicate.

Lawyers and law firms have a similar opportunity, although disruption in the legal space is much easier since most competitors pay little attention to brand experience. It's a huge hole just waiting to be filled.

SOME QUESTIONS TO ASK YOURSELF

Do you think that brand experience doesn't matter? Think again. Just consider your own consumer vetting and buying experiences. With greater access to information and greater availability of alternative products and services, odds are you've become a more discerning consumer over time. Your clients have too. So if you doubt the importance of the brand experience you offer to clients and prospects, ask yourself these questions:

1. Are you a better educated and tougher customer or client than you were ten years ago?

2. Do you simply accept, or carefully vet, broad claims of quality and expertise made by brands before buying what they are selling?

3. Does your level of scrutiny rise based on the importance of the outcome you are seeking?

4. Do you remain loyal to product and service providers that disappoint you, or do you quickly search out substitutes?

5. Do you require more value for your purchase, more bang for your buck?

6. Are you quick to tell others about a poor experience, or do you keep your opinion to yourself?

PART FOUR

MARKETING YOURSELF
AS AN EXPERT

9

CONTENT MARKETING: BUILDING TRUST, LOYALTY AND RESPECT

"Click." Did you hear that? That "click" was in your reader's head. It's the proverbial light-bulb moment when something you wrote resonated and registered with your audience. Someone has taken notice. You've just formed a relationship.

That click? That's the sound of your content marketing working.

How Content Marketing Works

The first three parts of this book focused on the importance of developing (1) a narrow niche expertise, (2) telling a compelling brand story, and (3) providing a refined brand experience so that you can become a one-of-a-kind lawyer. Those who execute steps 1, 2 and 3 really well will experience an uptick in market awareness and new business opportunities.

But over time, momentum will slow, inertia will take hold, and there will be a reversion to the mean. Selling is still required to sustain and expand existing relationships, and to develop new ones. But rest easy — cold calling, glad-handing and small talk are not required. At least not in the traditional sense.

WHAT IS CONTENT MARKETING?

There are many definitions of content marketing but one of the best, and most succinct, is from the Content Marketing Institute:

> Content marketing is a strategic approach focused on creating and distributing valuable, relevant, and consistent content to attract and retain a clearly defined audience — and, ultimately, to drive profitable customer action.

> Content marketing's purpose is to attract and retain customers by consistently creating and curating relevant and valuable content with the intention of changing or enhancing consumer behavior. It is an ongoing process that is best integrated into your overall marketing strategy, and it focuses on owning media, not renting it.

> Basically, content marketing is the art of communicating with your customers and prospects without selling.

(http://contentmarketinginstitute.com/2012/06/content-marketing-definition/.)

Implicit in step 1 is the principle that consumers of legal services desire, above all else, expertise. Unless expertise can be conveyed and validated through referral or reputation, it must be demonstrated through thought leadership expressed in the marketplace of ideas (i.e., content marketing). Generating and disseminating compelling content builds trust and awareness, and positions the content creator as an expert. It's the "long game" with a focus on relationship building, not the hard sell.

Here's how it works. We all have an orbit, or sphere of influence, that consists of people, companies and organizations that we interact with. Content is like gravity. It keeps contacts in your orbit. Those who become aware of you stay aware of you as a result of your content. Those not within your orbit move into it after becoming exposed to your content. Sharing content is also a respectful, thoughtful way to remain engaged with and keep former clients in your orbit during gaps between engagements.

When someone who is in your orbit experiences a problem or has an opportunity in an area that you have written on, you'll be high on that

person's list as someone who possesses the requisite expertise to help overcome the problem or seize the opportunity. While your reader may not be ready to act immediately, continued thought leadership will keep you top of mind, and when the time is right the relationship will shift from reader/writer to client/attorney.

Writing is not only critical in client generation, but also in client retention. Like in any relationship, at some point the grass on the other side can start to look greener to a client. Writing in an attorney-client relationship is like romance in a marriage. It keeps things fresh. It keeps things interesting. And it keeps the relationship strong. It's harder for a client to get a wandering eye if you're continually adding value to the relationship through your thought leadership.

Generate and share content. Keep contacts in your orbit. When an opportunity arises, you'll be top of mind. It's as simple as that. But it's not that easy.

The Rise of Wisdom Marketing

Several years ago, content marketing was a trend. Create content, push it out into the marketplace of ideas, and you'd be at the leading edge of marketing evolution. Early adapters of content marketing tactics, like any trendsetters, won style points for simply engaging in the activity.

But content marketing is now ubiquitous. And with ubiquity comes saturation. That's where we're at today. Just as the influx of cheap knockoffs signals the end of a fashion trend, today's saturated and soggy content market heralds the end of "Content Marketing Phase 1.0."

So what's next? Clearly "doing" content marketing is no longer enough. Good content is better, but insufficient. "Content Marketing Phase 2.0" requires more. It requires deep insights, education, substance and thoughtfulness. It places a premium on quality. It requires wisdom. Now and in the future, only those who impart wisdom through their content will build relationships on a foundation of trust, loyalty and mutual respect with their audiences.

But these relationships must be nurtured by giving of oneself. If you expect audiences to give you their attention, you must first give them your wisdom. Shallow thoughts and timid analysis are like mindless small talk. To form relationships, one must blaze new ground and inspire audiences. Those who do so will be at the leading edge of wisdom marketing.

An example is in order.

Almost all lawyers who blog struggle with topic selection. It's often not a problem of too few topics to write about — indeed the legal landscape is vast — but too many. For a lawyer who doesn't give much thought to his blog in the two-week interim between writing posts, an overabundance of possible topics can be paralyzing. There's a desire to write something new and interesting, but the two hours allotted on the to-do list for this task is simply not enough time to come up with a fresh take. So the lawyer cozies up in his comfort zone.

Enter "the fallback" post: the case law update. There is an important place for case law updates in legal blogs. Although I believe this content staple is overrepresented in most blogs, there is no doubt that a lawyer who keeps his audience abreast of developments in the law provides some value. But it's often not enough to justify the effort. Providing *content* is simply summarizing the opinion or statute. Imparting *wisdom*, however, involves thinking more deeply about the implications of the opinion.

Unless a lawyer maintains a "check the box" blog, a prop intended simply to maintain an online presence with minimal effort, the objective of a blog should be to showcase expertise and create differentiation. The way that most lawyers draft case updates does neither.

The typical case update follows the same pattern:

• A headline that mentions case name, possibly the legal question or topic at issue, and the outcome of case (*e.g.*, Supreme Court Rules in First Amendment Case of *Reed v. Town of Gilbert)*

• An opening paragraph that says pretty much the same thing as the headline, plus a link to the opinion

• A factual and procedural background section

• A summary of the court's analysis

In many ways, this format tracks that of most legal briefs. And I guess that's to be expected. That's how lawyers were trained to write, and instinct kicks in particularly when writing about case law. The problem is that when you're writing a brief, you're writing for a judge. Judges rule based on precedent. So a two-paragraph soliloquy from Justice Kennedy, while perhaps appropriate for a brief, likely has no place being pasted into a blog post. That's because unlike a judge, your readers aren't guided by precedent. What matters to them is real-world relevance.

An effective case update blog post, therefore, primarily addresses implications rather than simply conveying factual information.

In June 2015, the Supreme Court decided the Reed case mentioned above. It was a First Amendment case in which the Court ruled that an Arizona town's sign ordinance was "content based" and subject to "strict scrutiny."

Many lawyers and law firms wrote blog posts about this case. Most spent the first 500 words summarizing the facts and the next 500 explaining the legal opinion. Some wrapped up with a few sentences about the case's bigger picture impact. Few got any mileage out of their efforts. If the goal is to stand out, you have to stand out. The Reed case has many important implications for municipalities and other law/ordinance-making bodies. Most readers don't care what the justices wrote; they care about how what they wrote impacts *them*.

So instead of a case summary of the typical variety, a more effective approach would be to skip the lengthy summary — readers can find that information anywhere — and craft a post that explains to readers the "Five Action Steps Municipalities Should Take Now…" or the "Three Most Important Lessons Municipalities Should Learn…" related to the decision. Such a post would address the facts and law in a single introductory paragraph, then dive deep into the case's implications.

To differentiate in the online marketplace of ideas, zig when everyone else is zagging. But to truly zig, it means that you need to work a little harder and stay disciplined about the cases you write about. Start by choosing an industry you specialize in, and focus your case updates exclusively on how decisions impact that industry, including opportunities to exploit and risks to avoid. Your blog content may become relevant to a smaller audience as a result, but by directly and effectively addressing their needs, it will be a more engaged, interested and loyal audience.

Odds are that if you are taking the typical approach to case updates, not many people are reading them — there's too much competition for an audience that doesn't really care about your summary anyway. So flip the script and focus on what cases mean — in real-world, practical business terms — for your audience.

This book focuses primarily on one form of content marketing: writing. While I believe that writing is a great foundation for most robust content marketing efforts, it's certainly not the only way to reach and build an audience. Lawyers are creatively using video, podcasts, information graphics, SlideShare decks and many other content formats to get their message out. There is no shortage of outlets for good content. The lessons in this section are geared toward written content marketing, but are broadly applicable to whichever content format you choose to use. The point is to get really good, thoughtful content into the hands, eyes and ears of your audiences to win their hearts and minds. And ultimately their business.

How to Do It

"Write article for trade publication" languishes at the bottom of far too many lawyers' to-do lists. Lawyers can write, so why don't they? It's probably for the same reason people don't exercise every day — it's hard and requires lots of discipline. It's also a non-billable task that is easy to defer (and defer, and defer …). There's no secret formula to consistently writing good content. You just have to commit to it. Here are five tips:

1. Shut down the distractions. Disable email notifications, close Internet browsers, shut the door. Sit in the chair and prioritize your writing time.

2. Just let it rip. Don't try to edit as you go. Get words on the page, sleep on it and edit the next day.

3. Take notes. Write about issues that come up during the course of your day, week or month. Many people agonize over what to write about, blaming "writer's block" for lack of production. To overcome this hurdle, simply be more mindful throughout the day and take notes as you go. Every interaction you have, every matter you work on and every article you read contains nuggets of wisdom to write about.

4. Get it out there. Don't be afraid to compete in the marketplace of ideas. You're smart and have a point of view, so share it. Use the publishing resources your firm provides — website, blog, e-newsletters. Publish on LinkedIn. Find a trade publication in need of content. There's huge demand among publishers for good content; it just takes a little effort to find the right fit to reach your audience.

5. Stick with it for at least 30 days. It's easy to be habitual for a week. It's more challenging to plow forward for two or three weeks. Once you can get over that hump, though, it gets much easier. Hang in there and achieve some success (you will), and content creation will soon become an indispensable, inviolate part of your daily or weekly routine. Words will come, then insights, then invaluable wisdom that blazes new intellectual ground and gets you noticed.

How Often and How Much

Fresh content is like a bowl of fresh fruit. It looks great, is easily shared and (with the exception of that occasional mealy peach or mundane article) is a real crowd-pleaser. But content, like fruit, quickly loses its shine. Just as regular trips to the market are required to replenish your fruit supply, fresh content must be regularly generated to compete in the marketplace of ideas. While this analogy is quickly becoming over-ripe, it identifies a challenge that many lawyers and law firms face — the ability to create a sustained, interesting and effective content marketing initiative across numerous platforms.

Smart, savvy and skilled lawyers have the ability to crank out lots of great content. The challenge, though, is harnessing these resources. Client work, new business pitches and administrative work often get in the way, and that blog post that needs to be written languishes like a rotten banana (sorry — couldn't resist one more).

Here are the rules of thumb on how much and how often to write:

• If you're maintaining a blog, do at least one post per week, preferably two. One should be original content. The other can be a link to, and bit of commentary on, a news item or analysis that is of interest to you and your audience. Generally speaking, blog posts should be limited to 500 words or less.

• For longer pieces, shoot for one per month. Depending on where it's being published, 800-1,500 words is a good length. Unless your firm provides you with a platform (such as a newsletter or quarterly publication), you also will need to find a place to publish your article. Fortunately, many websites and trade publications are happy to publish thoughtful pieces.

WRITE THE BOOK ON IT

One of the biggest challenges lawyers face when pitching new business is effectively and authentically explaining to prospective clients why they are any better situated to help solve a specific problem than the multitude of other smart, hardworking lawyers out there. There are few better answers to the question "Why should I hire you to deal with this issue?" than "I wrote the book on it."

In many ways, getting a book published on a particular topic is the Holy Grail of content marketing. Nothing signifies expert status more effectively and more quickly. Just ask John Trentacosta, partner in Foley & Lardner's Detroit office, who focuses his practice in the automotive industry.

As a young lawyer, John began working in the automotive industry as the modern-day tiered supply chain came into existence. At that time, companies began focusing more intently on their contracting practices, including the terms and conditions included in purchase and supply contracts, and how those terms interact with the dictates of the Uniform Commercial Code (the "UCC"). Not only was this John's area of practice, but he was genuinely interested in the issues involved with the automotive supply chain.

While researching case law, it occurred to John that it was very inefficient not to have a single source that addressed the contract case law concerning the manufacturing industry. Being an enterprising young lawyer, John decided to take up the challenge himself.

After doing a bit of digging, he learned that other states had similar treatises, and so he approached the Institute of Continuing Legal Education (a Michigan provider of legal education and resources) about creating something similar in Michigan. His efforts resulted in him editing and contributing as an author of *Michigan Contract Law* (first published in 1998). He was also co-author and general editor of *Michigan Legal Forms-Uniform Commercial Code*, and has published numerous articles on UCC issues and commercial litigation in various legal and other trade publications.

According to John, being a published author on an issue of significance is "a great calling card" into the world of in-house counsel. It establishes instant credibility and leads to other opportunities. After publishing his first book, John experienced a big uptick in the number and quality of opportunities to write and speak, further exposing him to his target markets and burnishing his reputation. In other words, being published has a multiplier effect.

FROM SCRATCH — HOW A LAWYER BUILT A PRACTICE ONE BLOG POST AT A TIME

Mark Herrmann is the Vice President and Deputy Chief Counsel–Litigation and Employment at Aon. Previously he was a partner at Jones Day. He's also a piercing, witty and prolific writer, who has authored books and publishes articles frequently on websites such as Above the Law (www.abovethelaw.com).

When he was still at Jones Day, he was confronted with a challenge: How to establish a practice — drug and device product liability — for the firm, from scratch?

His solution: Get known. In an excellent Above the Law article entitled "Inside Straight: Building a Practice — a Case Study," Mark describes the technique as "Get famous. Make contact. Repeat."

The best way to get famous according to Mark? Writing is a key component of his strategy. As he explained to me, "The only way to establish your reputation is to write things that are interesting."

In addition to writing articles for outside publications, Mark started the Drug and Device Law Blog (http://druganddevicelaw.blogspot.com) with a co-blogger from another firm. This was in 2006 — while lawyer blogs seem ubiquitous now, at the time Mark was venturing into relatively uncharted territory.

"At first we were writing for ourselves," Mark explained. But he kept at it, publishing a post a day. After three years, they were generating 30,000 to 40,000 page views per month. Not only was Mark generating significant business for the firm's new practice, but his writing efforts were also making him even more "famous" in the field.

In 2009, Oxford University Press contacted Mark and his co-blogger about the prospect of writing a book on the defense of drug and device cases. Good content begets good content marketing opportunities.

Mark's advice for aspiring lawyer content marketers is to let one's personality shine through. He believes that most firms are overly cautious and "playing defense" when it comes to content marketing, which "sucks all the life" out of their content.

Unlock Writer's Block: How to Choose Good Topics

One of the great story lines from the movie *Caddyshack* is Carl Spackler's (Bill Murray) epic battle with the pesky golf course gopher. While the gopher proved to be a tougher adversary than Spackler expected, and ultimately outwitted the hapless greenskeeper, Spackler learned a few important lessons in his quest to rid Bushwood of the "varmint." One of them — which I discuss below — actually has relevance to this subject. So I've got that goin' for me, which is nice.

Alas, as much as I'd like to devote this space to making tortured *Caddyshack* analogies, we're really here to discuss how content marketing helps lawyers establish expertise and build books of business. So you're ready to write. But what should you write about?

Gophers or General Counsel: Know Your Audience

First, be purposeful and intentional about determining the audience you are writing for. Building credibility through content marketing does little good unless you're focused on the right people.

So how to go about this? Simply follow an old axiom, one that Spackler adopted in his futile gopher hunt: Know your audience. "My foe, my enemy, is an animal. And in order to conquer an animal, I have to think like an animal, and — whenever possible — to look like one. I've gotta get inside this guy's pelt and crawl around for a few days."

Spackler was hunting gophers, you're hunting clients, but the principle is the same. Know your audience, what makes them tick and what they care about. Then let the "hunt" begin.

A Conversation, Not a Lecture

The primary objective of content marketing is to build reputation and project expertise in the marketplace of ideas. Done well, content marketing raises your profile and helps nail down business opportunities. A prerequisite of any content marketing initiative, therefore, is developing content that clients and potential clients consider valuable and interesting. In other words, content they want to read and that they learn something from.

There are two ways to approach this. First, you can make an educated guess based on your experience and expertise as to what content to produce. This is not an unreasonable, nor ineffective, approach, and is the one that most legal content marketers adopt. The problem is that you may not know whether the topics you choose address the needs and desires of your intended audiences.

The second approach — which should be a fundamental building block of any effective content marketing program — is to elicit feedback, both before launching, and in the midst of, your content marketing initiative. Ask your audience what they are interested in. Not only will this lead to good topics, but it will help you craft a story — rather than a dry analysis — around the business challenges your clients face.

By having a two-way conversation with members of your audience, you'll make them feel like they are part of the process, and they will be invested in your content.

While there's no secret recipe for engaging your audience, there are a number of tactics that work well. Some lawyers and law firms do a great job of eliciting feedback from clients. If you have an active client feedback process already established, simply add content exploration to the mix of topics discussed. A less formal, but equally effective approach, is to ask questions in the midst of routine interactions — lunch meetings, status calls and networking events — that reveal insights into the issues that keep members of your target audience up at night.

Your audience is a potent source of ideas for your content. Whatever approach you take, just be consistent and thoughtful. Otherwise, in the immortal words of Judge Smails, "You'll get nothing and like it!"

Insight Mining Your Matters

Some of the best content ideas hide in plain sight. They reside in the emails, pleadings, documents and time entries of every lawyer at every firm. Deals and disputes are more than "matters," they're stories full of lessons others can learn from. To come up with content gold, simply mine insights from your matters.

Legal matters consist of fact patterns that must be gathered and understood. Then those facts must be analyzed in the context of relevant case law, statutes and regulations. While the specific circumstances of a particular matter are obviously unique and confidential, chances are that many other clients, or potential clients, of your firm have dealt or will deal with a similar scenario. And they can benefit from your experience, expertise and insights on the issue. But if you don't get your ideas out there in front of them, how are they to know that you're the right person to solve their problem?

Probably the most challenging aspect of insight mining is not coming up with topic ideas, but capturing them in an organized fashion for later use in your content marketing efforts. Whether you use a cloud-based note-taking app, or a simple pen and notepad, it's critical to record your ideas so that they'll be at your fingertips for later use.

"Newsjacking"

"Newsjacking" is content marketing jargon for a technique that generates great content ideas. Author David Meerman Scott coined the term, which he describes as "the process by which you inject ideas or angles into breaking news, in real-time, in order to generate media coverage for yourself or your business."

By staying on top of breaking industry news, court decisions, and new statutes and regulations, and adding your unique perspective, you can position yourself as a thought leader.

There a few things to keep in mind, though, when newsjacking. First, be ready. Anticipate news (for example, keep an eye on when the Supreme Court will be issuing opinions) so that your analysis is one of the first to hit the content marketplace. Second, be fast but not too fast. Be mindful not to jump in too quickly, which can lead to getting the facts wrong. Third, be cautious about controversy. Newsjacking should be done in good taste. Consider how your community and your audience may react to a particular topic before posting something; the last thing you want is for your attempt to generate positive PR to turn into a crisis PR situation.

Technology Alone Is Not the Answer

Many great content marketing technology tools are available. While some believe that technology is the key to building a great content marketing platform, in reality it just makes the process more efficient. It's no substitute for hard work and human engagement, which are the true content marketing building blocks.

Know your audience. Engage the people who make up your audience to learn their interests. Then talk with them, not at them, in an authentic way through your content. That is the way to build a passionate audience.

Hit It Out of the Park

If you've engaged in content marketing in the past, or intend to in the future, it's important to understand how the playing field has changed. In the past, traffic to most blogs followed predictable patterns, trending up or down gradually depending on the frequency at which new posts were added. The makeup of a blog's audience was consistent, too. Some readers dropped off, and others got on board, but by and large an audience came back consistently for their content. Times have changed.

Instead of loyally consuming the content of one blog, or a small number of blogs, readers are picking and choosing the best content available to them, from a wide variety of sources. In other words, they're not looking for a blog to follow, they're looking for a blog post to read, regardless of its origin.

Rather than beginning their content journey at one specific blog, readers are starting with Google, social media, Attorney at Work, or curation sites like the National Law Review and JD Supra. They don't want to waste their time consuming your content to validate its worth; they want someone else to validate it for them. "Shares" and "Likes" on LinkedIn, and high rankings on Google, suggest that your content is worth reading.

So what to do in this new environment? There's a place for singles and doubles, but in order to drive big traffic you need to hit the occasional content home run.

Anyone who has maintained a blog for any period of time likely will have at least a couple of content home runs. These are the posts that consistently appear at the top of the analytics charts, even though they may have been written months or even years prior. They are "evergreen," meaning they are timeless. They consistently bring new visitors to a blog — visitors who then consume other content on the site. Content home runs provide compounding returns for one's investment of time and resources.

What does a home run post look like? They come in all shapes and sizes, but have a few things in common. The wisdom imparted and information provided is helpful and thoughtful. The writing is crisp and engaging. And the topic selection is sharp and strategic.

Reinvent. Reinvigorate. Repurpose Your Content.

Once you've got a hit on your hands, broaden its reach. An article dealing with a seller's remedies upon a breach of contract under the Uniform Commercial Code is good content, but a series of articles on the topic custom-tailored to particular industries is even better. While the remedies may be the same for automotive suppliers and consumer products manufacturers, the course of dealings, business practices and customs in different industries may be different. Instead of glossing over the unique characteristics of different industries by making your content more general, modify your content and make it more relevant to different audiences.

In other words, repurpose your content.

A substantive 1,500-word article can typically be repurposed up to a white paper or e-book, or repurposed down to a series of blog posts or infographics. A presentation can be given as a webinar. A blog post can be made into a podcast.

Start by looking backwards. Review your website analytics and social media reactions ("Shares," "Likes," etc.) to determine your most popular posts or articles. A good evergreen indicator is when an old post is still at the top of your charts months, or even years, later. See if you can update, or add a new perspective, to a popular piece of content, then consider ways in which that content can be repurposed into other formats. This is the "hub and spoke" approach to content marketing. The original piece of content is the "hub" and the "spokes" are the other content formats you use to extend its reach. Revisit, remix and reap the rewards of your best content.

Content marketing is not designed to, nor will it, convert leads immediately. It's the long game, requiring continuous, long-term engagement. That's why evergreen content — home run content — that drives traffic over time is so important. It's the glue that holds a long-term content marketing strategy together, allowing it to pay dividends over time.

10

EXPERIMENT YOUR WAY TO MARKETING SUCCESS

Okay, so you have the essential elements in place. You've chosen a narrow area of expertise to pursue and have committed to building your personal brand. You've sharpened your brand experience, and started publishing thought leadership. You're finding that some things are working better than others. You've got a plan in place.

But the market is dynamic and changing, and you must be too. While the foundation for building your practice may be solid, the specific tactics you engage in to stay at the top of your game must evolve as new challenges present themselves. This requires flexibility, not rigidity.

Planning Is a Means Not an End

Business plans. Marketing plans. Professional development plans. The hard drives and filing cabinets of lawyers are littered with them. For some, developing a plan is a worthwhile exercise and a means to a desired end: business development and marketing success. But for many others, the planning process becomes an end in itself. The essential next step — action — is never taken.

Why Planning Often Leads to Inaction

Inaction can result from an overly ambitious plan that doesn't take into account time constraints. It may stem from poor planning that doesn't align with your particular strengths and weaknesses. For example, an introverted attorney who develops a marketing plan that includes numerous speaking and networking events is unlikely to act on that plan.

Whatever the reason, planning isn't for everyone.

Marketing plans are like New Year's resolutions. They contain a series of goals for the year and subgoals for the month, with associated action steps to help achieve the goals. Sounds simple enough.

But like New Year's resolutions, marketing plans rarely work out so simply. We all know this from our experience, right? The time to take an action step comes, but you're too busy with the deposition or document review. Or the action is something you dread, so you procrastinate.

Next thing you know, a month or a quarter has passed. You recommit, dig deep for motivation, then get sidetracked again. You feel discouraged and decide to put the plan back in the filing cabinet. Better luck next year.

And there's the rub: By developing detailed and expansive marketing plans, many lawyers set themselves up for failure because their plans are not practical. Instead of celebrating whatever marketing successes are achieved, and focusing energy on what works, they focus instead on what wasn't accomplished.

The other big problem with planning is that it forces us to make decisions with imperfect information. Our time and resources are finite, so which activities and tactics should be included in a marketing plan? If we knew the outcome of an activity, planning would be easy. But, of course, we don't, and paralysis often sets in.

Experiment Instead

Approaching marketing without a written plan doesn't mean you won't be actively engaged in marketing activities. It simply means you'll stop being limited — or paralyzed, even — by your plan.

Instead of planning, experiment. By experimenting, you'll learn what works, what you enjoy and what adds value to your current and prospective client relationships. As a result, you'll be able to align your marketing efforts with your strengths.

You'll also have the flexibility to make adjustments based on the results (or lack thereof) of your efforts. No need to agonize over progress tracking or action steps — just get after it. If you like to write, write. If you like to network, network. Follow your marketing passion and take action. If an activity is working, do more of it. If it's not working, stop. If you're operating according to a plan, there is often a tendency to stick with the plan for far too long, results notwithstanding.

That's not to say that some experiments don't come at a cost. You'll spend time and resources conducting a marketing experiment that results in failure, but you'll walk away from the experience wiser, and your next experiment will benefit from your new perspective.

A year is too long to stick with anything that's not working, so don't wait until it's time to create next year's plan to adjust your marketing activities. Become more nimble by experimenting.

Go Bird by Bird

One of the biggest issues with planning is that it can be overwhelming — it's easy to be ambitious on paper, but in practice that ambition can lead to paralysis. The same can be true of experimentation, especially if the proposed activity takes you out of your comfort zone. The key is to take it step by step.

There is a great little book by author Anne Lamott, called *Bird by Bird: Some Instructions on Writing and Life*. It contains many lessons on creative thinking and ways to approach your work. One of my favorite passages deals with the issue of paralysis — specifically, how to overcome the tendency we all have to get overwhelmed by the enormity of the task or challenge we are facing. Here's Lamott's advice, gleaned from a childhood family experience:

Thirty years ago my older brother, who was ten years old at the time, was trying to get a report on birds written that he'd had three months to write, which was due the next day. We were out at our family cabin in Bolinas, and he was at the kitchen table close to tears, surrounded by binder paper and pencils and unopened books on birds, immobilized by the hugeness of the task ahead. Then my father sat down beside him, put his arm around my brother's shoulder, and said, "Bird by bird, buddy. Just take it bird by bird." (Anne Lamott, *Bird by Bird: Some Instructions on Writing and Life*. New York: Anchor, 1995.)

We all want change to happen *right now*. But it doesn't work that way. You have to put in the work. Because the amount of change we seek often overwhelms us, we procrastinate and equivocate.

But by doing something — consistently, habitually — change happens. Step by step, and action by action, your marketing activity will begin to build momentum. Little victories will pile up, which will soon turn into big results. You can't accomplish everything today, but you can accomplish something. Just take it bird by bird.

Aim for Progress Rather Than Perfection

The key takeaway is that there is no "one-size-fits-all" approach to legal marketing and business development. If planning works for you, keep planning. But for those seeking an alternative, try experimenting this year. Pick an activity to engage in this month and dive in. Write a blog post per week, or make 12 phone calls to clients, contacts and colleagues. Whatever marketing experiment you commit to, give it your all.

If you're doing something you're excited about, and in the process getting your name and expertise out there, good things will happen. Don't aim for perfection, aim for progress. Once you've learned through experimentation what works for you, then you'll be in a position to create a marketing plan that works for you.

GOOD GROWTH: THE RIGHT WAY TO GROW YOUR LAW PRACTICE

The focus of this book is growth — both personal and professional. Growth is good. The steps and strategies outlined in prior chapters — establishing a niche expertise, developing a compelling personal brand and a robust content marketing strategy — will lead to more clients, more revenue, more staff and more opportunities. Exciting stuff.

But growth — unbridled — can be dangerous. Things can get out of control. If you're not careful, your practice can get on a "bad growth" path that is, at best, counterproductive and, at worst, personally and professionally destructive.

Slow and Steady Wins the Race: A Model for Firm Growth

Becoming a one-of-a-kind lawyer requires thoughtful consideration and strategic action to build a practice that has good growth rather than bad growth.

Bad growth happens rapidly and unexpectedly. Many times lawyers and law firms don't realize they are on a bad growth trajectory until it's too late. There are many high-profile examples of the unraveling of fast-growth firms, such as Dreier LLP, which result in liquidation and indictments. But more common, if less spectacular, are instances where bad growth leads to anguish, stress and distraction for individual lawyers and small firms.

Many lawyers have experienced bad growth, most often in the form of difficult clients. For some, a difficult client is one that is unreasonably demanding. For others, it's a client that always pushes back on fees. You may not even be aware of the problems particular clients are causing if they act one way with you and another way with associates and staff. While there will always be difficult clients, the key is to limit their impact on your firm or practice.

If you have too many of the wrong type of clients, you may experience growth, but of the wrong variety.

That's why it's important to periodically stop and assess your client mix and business objectives. Rather than taking on whatever work comes in the door, strategically determine the type of clients you enjoy working with and the type of work that is interesting and profitable. Instead of selling your services, focus instead on aligning with the right types of clients. If parameters are set in advance, it makes it much easier to turn away work that is not the right fit.

An ad hoc approach to business development leads to bad growth. A more thoughtful one results in good growth.

The Ostrich Problem: An Impediment to Good Growth

Bad growth is often fueled by "The Ostrich Problem," which is how a group of psychologists in England describe the widespread tendency to avoid information that would inform us as to whether we are — or are not — making progress toward our goals. For example, someone may want to lose weight, but consciously avoids tracking daily calorie intake or stepping on a scale.

In a law firm setting, "The Ostrich Problem" may manifest as ignorance of associate billable hour write-offs, increasing age of accounts receivables, declining profitability, or lack of client diversification. Whatever the symptoms, the cause is often the same: fear.

The "Ostrich" researchers assert that monitoring progress conflicts with the "self-enhancement motive," which is the idea that people want to maintain a favorable view of themselves, and are fearful of information that would negatively impact that view. At some level, most lawyers experiencing bad growth know it, but refuse to gather or acknowledge the information that would confirm their lack of progress. Without information, there can be no planning. And without planning, there can be no forward progress. Ignorance may be bliss, but it's bad for the bottom line.

Establishing a Growth Plan

Adopting a strategic plan for growth helps fuel good growth. When you foster and sustain a manageable growth trajectory, you control your practice, rather than allowing it to control you. Instead of being reactive to the pressures of increased workflow, it's much better to stay a step ahead by hiring great people, acquiring appropriate office space, creating systems and policies, and implementing helpful technology in advance of the crush of new business.

One paradox of a good growth model is that it often results in — indeed requires — slow, purposeful growth. But once you have the right plan in place, it's much easier, and more profitable, to attract and retain new clients.

Onboarding New Clients

As discussed earlier, onboarding new clients is an essential element of creating a positive, memorable brand experience. It is also one of the most important steps in building a good growth practice. It's a process of engagement and discovery that helps you determine whether a potential new client is a right client.

Too often the only prerequisites to forming an attorney-client relationship (a difficult one to end) are a retainer check and engagement letter signature.

Onboarding constructs some speed bumps that slow down this process and help validate that the prospective client is a good fit. It involves conversations with clients about expectations, timelines and financial issues. It's also a chance for the client to get to know you and your firm.

Bad clients may be put off by this process. That's the point. Good clients will appreciate the opportunity to explore alignment and set expectations at the outset. It's a sign to the client that you and your practice are stable, mature and thoughtful in your approach to business. No one likes to find out halfway through an engagement that there were different expectations about objectives or pricing. Having those conversations up front will preempt uncomfortable ones down the road.

Pruning Clients

Beyond being more selective and thoughtful in developing new clients, good growth can be fueled by pruning your existing client base. Difficult clients can suck up all the oxygen in a room, consuming the energy and focus of a firm and its lawyers. Consequently, good clients feel neglected and leave, or at least pull back. That's why it's critical to carefully, responsibly and judiciously part ways with difficult clients.

Pruning is not easy and requires a change in mindset. Many lawyers cling to bad clients like a handhold on a sheer cliff out of fear of losing revenue. But "losing" a bad client frees up capacity — most importantly, mental capacity — to pursue better work and opportunities. Clinging to bad clients leads to bad growth, then stagnation and, ultimately, decline.

Parting ways with a difficult client is not a loss, it's a gain. It's much better to "shrink" and marshal resources around good client relationships that hold future promise.

Get On the Right Path

Progress monitoring, planning, onboarding and pruning are all key elements of a good growth plan. If you find yourself on a bad growth path, stop. Cut yourself some slack, because you are most definitely not alone. Armed with real data, start making some small changes that will result in big improvements in your practice. As you move forward and grow as a lawyer and build, or build upon, a book of business, it's critically important to have a foundation for good growth in place.

Conclusion

When you're in law school, it's easy to think that's the place to get an education. And it is, to an extent, although a relatively small one. As most lawyers quickly learn, trial by fire is the most common, if not the most effective, method used to train new lawyers. In fact, trial by fire never really ends during a lawyer's career — the stakes and the challenges just grow. In other words, in order to grow as a lawyer, you can never stop learning.

The beauty of living in the digital age is that information about almost anything is at our fingertips. There are no barriers to knowledge. Likewise, we can make our own knowledge available to the world. There are, therefore, no barriers to becoming an expert and projecting expertise to the marketplace other than the ones we construct ourselves. It's our desire for security and comfort that often leads to stagnation.

Expert lawyers at the pinnacle of their field are not those who think they know everything and have it all figured out. They suffer from the same insecurities that we all do, but those insecurities drive them to be better. They never stop learning, opening their minds to creative new ideas and polishing their skill sets. As John Wooden said, "It's what you learn after you know it all that counts."

Becoming an expert lawyer involves a continuous, repeatable cycle of learning, acting and adapting. It's a lifelong journey, not a single destination. In your own mind you may never get there, and that's not necessarily a bad thing. But if you put the work in — you'll find that, little by little, you'll make remarkable progress.

REFERENCES

- Teresa Amabile, *The Progress Principle: Using Small Wins to Ignite Joy, Engagement, and Creativity at Work* (Watertown, MA: Harvard Business Review Press, 2011).

- Clayton Christensen, Dina Wang, and Derek van Bever, "Consulting on the Cusp of Disruption" (*Harvard Business Review*, https://hbr.org/2013/10/consulting-on-the-cusp-of-disruption).

- Jim Collins, *How the Mighty Fall: And Why Some Companies Never Give In* (Jim Collins, 2009).

- Content Marketing Institute, www.contentmarketinginstitute.com.

- Howard Gardner, *Intelligence Reframed: Multiple Intelligences for t he 21st Century* (New York: Basic Books, 2000).

- Anne Lamott, *Bird by Bird: Some Instructions on Writing and Life* (New York: Anchor, 1995).

- Greg McKeown, *Essentialsim: The Disciplined Pursuit of Less* (New York: Crown Business, 2014).

- David Meerman Scott, *Newsjacking: How to Inject your Ideas into a Breaking News Story and Generate Tons of Media Coverage* (New York: Wiley, 2011).

- Amy Wrzesniewski, Yale School of Management, http://faculty.som.yale.edu/amywrzesniewski/.

We hope you enjoyed this Attorney at Work book.

Be sure to sign up for new content, updates and news on discounts from Attorney at Work. Attorney at Work delivers "one really good idea every day" via our free Daily Dispatch newsletter.

Subscribe at www.attorneyatwork.com/subscribe